Co

Introduction	5	Rice Bran Compress	36
		Rice Bran Pickles	37
Aduki Bean Rice	11	Rice Bran Plaster	38
Amasake	12	Rice Bread	39
Ame Kuzu Tea	13	Rice Kayu Bread	39
Barley Rice	14	Carolina Rice and	40
Soft Barley Rice	14	Wheat Bread	
Black Soybean Rice	15	Rice Cakes	41
Boiled Rice	16	Sweet Rice Cakes	41
Omo: African-Style Rice	16	Small Fried Rice Cakes	42
Chestnut Rice	17	Sweet and Savoury Rice	42
Congee	18	Cakes	42
Fermented Rice	19	Rice with Corn	43
Idli Steamed Bread	19	Rice Cream	44
Fermented Rice Drink	19	Rice Croquettes	45
Fried Rice	20	Wild Rice Croquettes	45
Fried Rice Balls	20	with a Mushroom-	
Baked Rice Balls	20	Onion Sauce	
Genshin Tea	21	Rice with Daikon Pickles	46
Ginger-Scallion-Rice Wine	22	Rice Drink	47
Compress		Fermented Rice Drink	47
Ginger Tea with Rice	23	Sweetened with	
Hato Mugi Rice	24	Barley Malt	
Millet Rice	25	Sprouted Oat-Rice Milk	47
Soft Millet Rice	25	Rice Fast	48
Mochi	26	Rice-Ginger Compress	49
Home-made	26	Rice Gomoku	50
Pan-fried	26	Rice Juice	51
Fried	27	Rice Liquid	52
in Bancha Tea	27	Rice with Lotus Seeds	53
in Miso Soup	28	Rice Soup with Lotus	53
Ohagi	29	Seeds	
Ojiya	30	Rice with Marinated	54
Pressure-Cooked Rice	31	Dried Daikon	
Raw Rice	33	Rice Milk	55
Rice Balls	34	Rice-Miso Plaster	56
Rice with Beans	35	Raw Rice Plaster	56

Rice Noodles	57
Rice Noodles in Broth	57
Rice Pack	58
Rice Porridge	59
Fresh Soft Porridge	59
Porridge with Leftover Rice	59
Miso Rice Porridge	60
Rice Porridge with Aduki Beans	61
Rice Porridge with Bancha Tea	61
Rice Porridge with Barley	62
Rice Porridge with Corn	62
Rice Porridge with Grated Daikon	62
Rice Porridge with Grated Lotus Root	62
Rice Porridge with Millet	63
Rice Porridge with Millet, Buckwheat, and Vegetables	63
Rice Porridge with Squash	64
Roasted Rice Porridge	64
Sweet Rice Porridge	64
Rice Powder	65
Rice Poultice	66
Rice Flour Poultice	66
Skin and Beauty Poultice	66
Rice Pudding	67
Amasake Pudding	67
Rice Soup	68
Brown Rice Soup	68
Thunder Tea Soup	68
Rice and Sweet Vegetables with Vinegar	70
Rice Syrup	71
Rice Tea	72
Roasted Rice Tea	72
Rice Tea with Aduki Beans, Dried Daikon, and Shiitake	72
Rice Tea with Dried Daikon, Daikon Leaves, and Shiitake	73
Rice Tea with Dried Daikon, Daikon Leaves, Shiitake, and Dried Lotus Root	73
Rice Tea with Dried Daikon, Kombu, and Shiitake	73
Rice Tea with Dried Daikon, Shiitake, and Cabbage	74
Rice Tea with Lotus Root	74
Rice with Green Tea	
Rice Vinegar	75
Sweet and Sour Sauce	75
Rice Water	76
Rice with Water-Sautéed Daikon and Daikon Leaves	77
Rice Wine	78
Mirin	78
Sake	78
Roasted Rice	79
Sprouted Rice	80
Sweet Rice	81
Sweet Rice	81
Sweet Rice Dumplings	81
Vegetable Sushi	82
White Rice	83
Wild Rice	84
Rice with Wild Rice	84
Popped Wild Rice	84
Appendix 1: Dietary Guidelines	85
Appendix 2: The Nutritional Benefits of Rice	88
Resources	91
About the Authors	92

108 Special Dishes, Drinks, Compresses, and Other Home Remedies

Healing with Rice

Alex and Gale Jack
Amberwaves™

Note to the Reader

The approach introduced in this book is educational, not medical, and incorporates traditional folk remedies and contemporary natural solutions for common ailments. Anyone with a serious illness or medical emergency is advised to seek the prompt attention of a physician or other professional.

If you have a personal experience that you would like to share with others using one of the methods in this book or a new remedy, please submit it to the address below for possible use in future publications. Corrections, suggestions, and other comments are also welcomed.

Dedicated to preserving natural and organic rice
for endless generations

Healing with Rice
© 2003 by Alex Jack and Gale Jack

All rights reserved. Printed in the United States of America. No part of this book may be used or reproduced in any manner whatsoever without written permission except in the case of brief quotations embodied in critical articles or reviews. For information, contact the publisher.

For further information on mail-order sales, wholesale or retail discounts, distribution, translations, and foreign rights, please contact the publisher:

Amberwaves™
P.O. Box 487
Becket, MA 01223, U.S.A.
Tel (413) 623-0012 • Fax (413) 623-6042
Email: info@amberwaves.org

1st Edition: September 2003
10 9 8 7 6 5 4 3 2 1

IBSN 0–9708913–4–2
Printed in the U.S.A.

INTRODUCTION

"Eat foods made from a variety of whole grains—such as whole wheat, brown rice, oats, and whole grain corn—every day."
—U.S. Dietary Guidelines for Americans

Rice Planet

Rice, the most widely consumed food on the planet, has been a staple in the human diet from time immemorial. It is hulled, milled, or processed into dozens of products, also making it the world's most versatile crop. Rice may date back to Pangaea, the single land mass, that broke into two supercontinents. About 20 to 30 million years ago, Northern and Southern strains of rice appear to have evolved separately in Asia and Africa. Rice experts have long dismissed wild rice as an unrelated annual grass. But new research from Minnesota's Center for Microbial and Plant Geonomics recently determined that North American wild rice, *Zizania aquatica*, and Asia rice, *Oryza sattiva*, are closely related, diverging from a common ancestor only about 1 million years ago.

The Buddha ate rice under a tree and attained enlightenment. Lao Tzu, Confucius, and Gandhi sang its praises. Leonardo da Vinci, Shakespeare, and Jefferson delighted in it. When he was ill, Charles Darwin recuperated on it. Rice has played a central role in world history, serving as the principal food for many ancient civilizations. In the middle ages, it came to Europe over the fabled Silk Road and contributed to the flourishing of the Renaissance. By way of Arabia and the Moors, rice also influenced Mediterranean culture. In pre-Columbian America, native peoples enjoyed wild rice from the Great Lakes to the Appalachias. Following the arrival of the Europeans, rice formed the foundation of slavery for 250 years until it was succeeded by cotton. In the 20th century, wars were fought in the ricefields of China, the Philippines, Korea, Vietnam, Laos, Cambodia, and other Asian countries, leading to an exodus of refugees who further spread a rice-based cuisine around the globe.

Today rice is grown in nearly every climate and environment (from Alaska to Australia) and is widely recognized as the foundation of a healthy, planetary cuisine. The 2000 edition of the U.S. government's dietary guidelines recommends that people "enjoy meals that have rice, pasta, tortillas, or whole grain bread at the center of the plate." The guidelines, which accompany the Food Guide Pyramid, also explain that eating whole grains may protect against many chronic diseases, including heart disease, certain types of cancer, diabetes, stroke, and osteoporosis. Obesity, high blood pressure, and high blood cholesterol are also listed as conditions that can be relieved with a balanced, grain-based way of eating.

As the new nutritional policy of the United States shows, ancient and modern medicine are converging. Scientific and medical research is confirming the benefits of traditional diets, cuisines, and home remedies that have been practiced for thousands of years. A summary of recent nutritional studies on the value of rice is included in the appendix along with dietary guidelines for a balanced vegetarian, vegan, and macrobiotic way of eating.

The material in this book is drawn from humanity's medicinal heritage and our studies, travels, and insights over the last several decades. It includes recipes and remedies from India, China, Japan, Vietnam, and other Asian countries, as well as Africa, Europe, the Middle East, and the Americas. As part of a balanced diet, we enjoy cooking whole grain rice fresh daily. For healing, we have used rice in many medicinal dishes, teas, and external applications and recommended them to our students, colleagues, and clients.

Healing with Rice

The recipes and home remedies presented in this book are simple, safe, and inexpensive. They are also effective. Unlike many drugs and pharmaceuticals that originate in the tropical rain forests, they do not have a destructive effect on the planet's ecosystem. Compared to many pills and medications, they can be prepared easily by anyone and bring healing back into the reach of the family.

Traditional medicine was based on polarity—or the balance of complementary opposites such as yin and yang—and an energetic understanding of life. In treating various conditions, substances were selected that had a complementary/opposite energy (for example, the use of plants to treat human beings). Moreover, foods that had a similar look or shape corresponded to particular organs. Thus for kidney troubles, beans that had the shape of the kidneys were recommended. For respiratory troubles, lotus roots shaped like the alveoli, or air sacs, of the lungs were traditionally eaten.

Rice shares many of the same qualities and characteristics of human beings. They both stand upright but adapt flexibly to the changing environment. They have deep roots that reach into the earth. They have antennae-like structures that attract invisible vibrations from the heavens. Rice nourishes mind, body, and spirit as a whole. Because it co-evolved with human beings over millions of years during an era of sustained glacial ice and cold, rice especially nourishes the kidneys and reproductive organs. It is not surprising that rice is a traditional symbol of fertility in East and West (where it is still showered on newlyweds to bring prosperity and a large family).

Compared to other grains, rice is also very compact and has no seam or line dividing it into halves as do wheat, oats, barley, and other grains. These qualities stimulate digestion, respiration, and unified thinking. In the Far East, the ideogram for *ki*, or life energy, depicts the steam rising from cooked rice. The symbol for peace, *wa*, combines rice and a stylized mouth, showing that ancient people intuitively knew that eating whole grains contributed to the development of a calm, peaceful mind.

Despite its light texture and quality, rice produces strong, energy, instills perseverance, and contributes to longevity. Rice retains its vitality almost indefinitely, and there are instances of seeds sprouting after thousands of years. We have been experimenting recently with rice propagated from seeds unearthed in an ancient tomb in Japan. This hardy, dryland rice comes in many hues and has strong, unifying energy. We are networking with farmers in many parts of the United States, as well as Japan, Russia, and Africa, who are growing heirloom rice and other crops. For medicinal preparations, these varieties are preferred, though organic rice grown in California, Arkansas, and other states is among the best, most nourishing rice in the world.

In addition to personal health, rice contributes to planetary health. Rice fields constitute the single largest sanctuary for wildlife in the world. Hundreds of species of birds, mammals, insects, amphibians, reptiles, and tiny fish live in the rice fields. In the Sacramento Valley of California, site of most organic rice production in the United States, one quarter of all migrating ducks, geese, and other waterfowl set down in the rice fields to glean grains left from the harvest.

Preparing Home Remedies

The material in this book includes 1) daily recipes that will help protect people in usual good health from sickness and disease, including regular pressure-cooked or boiled rice; 2) daily recipes that also have medicinal applications, including millet rice, barley rice, or rice with corn, that are suitable for everyone, but especially for those with pancreatic, liver, or heart problems respectively; and 3) medicinal preparations, including special dishes, teas, and compresses that are used only for healing purposes.

The last type (medicinal preparations) are recommended only for specific conditions and for a short time—from one to three days in many cases, to seven to ten days in other cases, to several months in still others. As a rule, it is more effective to stop a special drink or compress after a brief time and then let the stimulated organs work and adjust, and then repeat the remedy a few days, a week, or a few weeks later. By then, the condition has usually improved, so you don't need to take as much the second time. In the proper use of home remedies, less is more. Overuse of remedies—like overeating, even of good quality food—can cause imbalance.

It is especially useful to apply these methods when you have just started to change your diet, as the body's eliminatory processes are more active at this time. In the beginning, as the body adjusts to whole, natural foods, it begins to eliminate excess. We call this process *discharging.* In addition to normal eliminatory channels such as the urine and bowel movements, excess may be discharged through fever, coughing, or other abnormal channels. Some of the remedies serve to make the discharge process more comfortable or control its frequency and duration. But once again, be mindful. In the beginning, it is sometimes difficult to distinguish a worsening condition from a discharge. Please seek the advice and guidance of an experienced dietary counselor and/or medical professional.

When preparing home remedies, it is usually best to take them on an empty stomach, such as mid-morning or mid-afternoon or sometimes in the early evening. However, it is better not to eat or drink three hours before sleeping in order to allow for proper digestion. Of course, the amount of each remedy to be prepared, the frequency with which it is to be used, the number of days or weeks it should be taken, and the time it will take to heal or recover will differ from person to person. For serious conditions, professional guidance once again is necessary. Please see the Resource Section for information on counseling resources as well as recommended books, Internet sites, and mail order sources.

Getting Started

In preparing the recipes and remedies in this book, it is essential to obtain the highest quality organic rice available. In a temperate, four-season climate, such as most of North America, Europe, Russia, China, and Japan, *short-grain brown rice* is the standard for day to day health and vitality and gives the strongest energy. *Medium-grain brown rice* is suitable for occasional use, and *long-grain* or *basmati rice* gives a light, soothing energy that is especially relaxing in the summer or warmer regions. Specialty rices from Italy, France, Spain,

Bhutan, India, Thailand, Japan, and other countries are nice for special dishes and preparations, but for daily and most medicinal use we prefer organic rice from California or Arkansas. We use polished rice very sparingly, as noted in the section on "White Rice."

The two standard ways of preparing rice are pressure-cooking and boiling. Please start with these two basic methods, as they are used in making many of the other preparations. In setting up your kitchen, we recommend obtaining a pressure cooker; heavy ceramic cast-iron pot (for boiling); stainless steel saucepans, skillets, and other cookware; a *suribachi* (Japanese style earthenware mortar) and pestle for making special drinks and compresses; a wooden rice bowl or bucket to store rice; and an assortment of attractive rice bowls, serving dishes, and utensils, especially wooden rice paddles, spoons, and cooking chopsticks. Purchasing the highest quality cookware is an investment in your family's health and well being that will bring many healthful returns over the years.

Good quality natural water (from a spring, well, or filter) is also essential, along with natural unrefined sea salt that retains the minerals and trace elements in the ocean. We recommend a generic white sea salt that flows smoothly and does not clump (indicating that its mineral content is not too high). The quality of the fire used in cooking also shapes our daily health. Gas is the standard in most macrobiotic and environmentally conscious households today, giving a clean, even heat and steady vibration. However, wood, charcoal, or other natural fuel is also suitable. Strictly avoid microwave and electrical cooking that create chaotic energy, change the quality and vibration of the food, and may lead to harmful changes in blood, lymph, and other body chemistry. For healing purposes, fire quality cannot be overemphasized.

Shining Grace

We are deeply grateful to educator Michio Kushi and his late wife, Aveline, for helping to introduce organic brown rice to modern America and teaching society how to heal with rice and other essential foods. We also wish to express our thanks to other pioneers in the macrobiotic community, including George and Lima Ohsawa, Herman and Cornelia Aihara, and Shizuko Yamamoto; pioneer rice growers and organic manufacturers, including Lundberg Family Farms, Southern Brown Rice, and Eden Foods; Tim Johnson, president of the California Rice Commission; our colleagues Edward and Wendy Esko, Adelbert and Wieke Nelissen, Charles Millman and Patricia Price, John and Jeanette Kozinski, and many others; and our families, students, and friends.

We are especially grateful to Linda Norris, our dear friend and associate, and The NOAH Center in Great Barrington, Mass., for supporting our activities and making a generous contribution to help publish this volume.

This book is the first in a series on "Natural Home Remedies." Grown without harmful chemicals or preservatives, natural and organic food is preferable for daily health as well as medicinal preparations. Organic foods also do not contain genetically modified organisms (GMOs), nor are they irradiated—two indispensable qualities for using food as medicine today. Future volumes will present remedies using other whole grains; soups and broths; vegetables, salads, and pickles; beans and soy products; fruits, seeds, and nuts; teas and medicinal beverages; and compresses, poultices, and other external applications.

This book is published by Planetary Health/Amberwaves, a network of individuals, families, and communities devoted to preserving natural and organic rice, wheat, and other foods from genetic engineering and other environmental threats. It will be tragic if humanity's principal food is contaminated and this priceless healing legacy lost. We invite you to join with us in preserving this heritage for our children and all future generations.

As the new century began, scientists began unraveling the genetic codes of many species of organisms. The first two genomes to be mapped were those for human beings and rice. In view of the spiral evolution of humanity and whole grains, this coincidence is especially meaningful. Like twin strands of DNA, the history and destiny of *Homo sapiens* is intertwined with amber waves of grain. We feel strongly that rice—the grain whose origins reach back to the time when the world was one—will flourish someday as the principal staple in North America and its popularity spread across Europe, Russia, and other regions. We foresee endless fields, gardens, and urban plots of multicolored rice and other whole grains filling the planetary landscape, unifying humanity, helping to restore the natural environment, and contributing to the age-old dream of enduring health and peace.

> Alex and Gale Jack
> Becket, Massachusetts
> June 1, 2003

ADUKI BEAN RICE

- Beneficial for kidney and bladder problems; ovarian, prostate, and other reproductive problems; infertility; retardation; leukemia; excess animal food

Aduki beans are small red beans. Native to Japan and the Far East, they are now grown in the United States and other countries. For daily use, the American variety is fine. For medicinal use, the Asian adukis are stronger. This dish is also known as Red Rice and is featured on New Year's and other festive occasions in the East. It attracts luck, happiness, and fertility. However, it can also be used for healing. Aduki beans are especially beneficial for the urinary system and reproductive functions. In the event that the kidneys are tight from excessive use of salt or salty foods (a major cause of kidney stones), kombu may be used in seasoning the rice and beans. Aduki bean rice is also helpful to counter heavy dairy or meat consumption.

1. Wash $1/2$ cup of aduki beans, place in a saucepan with 2 cups of water, and boil for 10 to 15 minutes. Don't overboil or the deep red color of the liquid will be lost.
2. After boiling, let the mixture cool to lukewarm.
3. Wash 3 cups of brown rice and place in a pressure cooker.
4. Add the beans to the rice.
5. Add the liquid in which the beans cooked with enough additional water to equal 5 cups.
6. Add a pinch of salt or a 1-inch square of kombu.
7. Turn the heat to high. Place the cover on the pressure cooker and bring up to pressure.
8. When the pressure is up, reduce the heat to medium-low. Place a flame deflector under the pressure cooker and cook 50 minutes.
9. Remove the cover when the pressure is down completely.
10. Let the aduki rice sit for 5 minutes to loosen the grains on the bottom of the pot.
11. Remove, place in a serving bowl, and serve.

- Variations: For a more digestible dish, soak the rice and beans together for 3 to 4 hours, or overnight, before cooking.
- For retardation or leukemia, use kombu instead of salt in seasoning.

AMASAKE

- Beneficial to relax and satisfy the cravings for a sweet taste; tight, stressful conditions; depression, hypoglycemia, and mood swings; overweight; grinding of teeth

Amasake is a delicious rice beverage. It is made from *koji*, a fermented grain and sweet brown rice, a glutinous variety of rice. Traditionally it is made fresh at home, but today it is widely available ready made in natural foods stores. Cooked and processed into a thick liquid, amasake is an excellent source of high quality, grain-based complex sugars. It is customarily eaten hot or cold and may be used as a sweetener in puddings and other recipes. In this case, it is often thickened with kuzu root. The following recipe is for home-made amasake, which has the strongest healing power.

1. Wash 4 cups of sweet brown rice, drain, and soak in 5 to 6 **cups of** water overnight.
2. Place rice and soaking water in a pressure cooker and bring to pressure. Lower heat and cook for 45 minutes.
3. Turn off heat and allow to sit in pressure cooker for another 45 minutes.
4. When cooled, mix $1/2$ cup of koji into the rice with your hands.
5. Transfer the mixture to a glass bowl (avoid metal), cover with a wet towel or cloth, and place near an oven, radiator, or other source of warmth.
6. Allow to ferment 8 hours or overnight, occasionally stirring the mixture to melt the koji.
7. After fermenting, place amasake in a pan and bring to a boil, adding water if necesscary. When bubbles appear, turn off the heat and allow to cool
8. Refrigerate in a glass bowl or jar and tightly seal. It will keep for several weeks.
9. To serve as a beverage, stir the amasake and place in a saucepan with a pinch of sea salt and enough water for desired consistency.
10. Bring to a boil and serve hot or allow to cool and serve chilled.

- When used as a sweetener in puddings, pastries, and other dishes, add the amasake directly or blend first until smooth.
- For children under 1 year, you may omit the salt.

AME KUZU TEA

- Beneficial to relax and satisfy the cravings for a sweet taste; tight, stressful conditions; depression, hypoglycemia, and mood swings; overweight; menstrual cramps; grinding of teeth

Ame kuzu tea can help calm and soothe a tight, contracted condition caused by too much stress, tension, or hard baked foods, salty foods (chips and crackers), or animal products. Kuzu is the powdered root of the kuzu plant, a prolific vine known in the American South as kudzu. It is a natural high-quality thickener and used in many medicinal drinks and preparations, as well as regular cooking instead of corn starch, baking powder, or other highly refined product. This tea is sweetened with brown rice syrup, brown rice malt, or other natural sweetener.

1. Dissolve 1 level tablespoon of kuzu in 2 or 3 tablespoons of cold water.
2. Add 1 cup of cold water.
3. Add 1 to 2 teaspoons of brown rice syrup or rice malt to the dissolved mixture.
4. Bring to a boil over a medium heat.
5. Stir continually to avoid lumping until the mixture turns transparent.
6. Reduce the flame as low as possible and simmer for a few minutes.
7. Serve while hot.

BARLEY RICE

- Beneficial for general good health; liver and gallbladder problems

Barley cooked with rice makes for a lighter, more relaxing dish. It is especially helpful to counter tight, contractive conditions and to give a calm, peaceful mind.

1. Wash 2 cups brown rice and $1/2$ cup of barley and place in a pressure cooker.
2. Add a pinch of sea salt, cover, and bring up to pressure.
3. Cook for 45 to 50 minutes.
4. Let sit for 5 minutes and allow the pressure to come down naturally.
5. Gently remove from the pot and serve.

Soft Barley Rice

This porridge is very soothing and may be made fresh or prepared with leftover grain.

1. If preparing fresh, follow above recipe, using 4 to 5 cups of water per cup and a pinch of sea salt per cup of grain.
2. If using leftover grain, place in a saucepan, add about $1/3$ to $1/2$ the volume of water, and cook for about 15 to 20 minutes until soft.

BLACK SOYBEAN RICE

• Beneficial for general health and for breast, prostate, ovarian, and other hormone-related conditions

Black soybean rice is a substantial dish, traditionally prepared on both festive occasions and on funeral days (probably because of its dark color). High in phytoestrogens, whole soybeans are especially protective against hormone-related disorders in both men and women. Black soybeans are less fatty and more digestible than yellow soybeans.

1. Place $1/2$ cup black soybeans on a clean, damp towel and rub them to remove any impurities. Do not wash the soybeans or their delicates skins will come off.
2. Dry-roast the soybeans in a skillet for several minutes, stirring constantly to avoid burning. When the insides of the beans are slightly brown, they are done.
3. Clean and wash 2 cups brown rice.
4. Combine the beans and rice in a pressure-cooker and add 3 to 3 $1/2$ cups water and 1/4 teaspoon sea salt.
5. Bring to a slow boil, about 15 to 20 minutes, cover, and bring up to pressure.
6. When pressure is up, place a flame deflector under the pot and let cook for 50 to 60 minutes.
7. When done, turn off heat and let the pressure come down naturally for about 5 minutes.
8. Remove the rice and beans, garnish with chopped scallions or parsley, and serve.

BOILED RICE

- Beneficial for general health and vitality; digestive problems, including stomach troubles, constipation, and diarrhea; better circulation and cardiovascular health; nervous conditions; and general natural immunity from disease

Boiled rice is the standard way of preparing rice in many parts of the world. It is traditionally made in sturdy cast-iron or ceramic pots with heavy lids. For medicinal use, a heavy crock pot or other earthenware vessel is preferred for boiling. However, an ordinary stainless steel saucepan is perfectly acceptable. Avoid aluminum, copper, or other lighter metals that may leave trace elements in the food.

1. Wash 2 cups of brown rice (short, medium, or long-grain) and place in a heavy pot or saucepan.
2. Add 4 cups of water and 2 pinches of sea salt or a 1-inch square of kombu and cover with a lid.
3. Bring to a boil, lower, the flame, and simmer for about 40 to 50 minutes or until all the water has been absorbed.
4. Remove and serve.

- Variation: soaking the rice overnight or several hours before cooking makes this easier to digest.

Omo or African-Style Rice

Omo, or plain boiled rice, is the traditional staple in West Africa.

1. Bring 4 cups of salted water to a boil.
2. Wash 3 cups long-grain brown rice in cold water and add to boiling water.
3. Add $1/8$ cup of sesame or other plant oil (optional).
4. Bring to a boil, stir with a wooden spoon, and cover with a tight-fitting lid.
5. Reduce heat to low and simmer for 20 minutes.
6. Remove from heat and let sit, covered, for 5 to 10 minutes.

CHESTNUT RICE

- Beneficial for general health and for pancreatic, stomach, and spleen problems

Chestnut rice is very sweet and delicious. It will help prevent cravings for simple sugars and stabilize blood sugar levels. It is especially enjoyed by women and girls of all ages.

1. Soak $1/2$ cup chestnuts for several hours.
2. Remove as much of the brown outer husk of the chestnuts as possible.
3. Wash 2 cups brown rice.
4. Layer the rice and chestnuts in a pressure cooker, add 4 to 5 cups water, and a pinch of sea salt, and bring up to pressure.
5. Cook for 45 to 50 minutes.
6. Remove from the flame and let set for 5 minutes until the pressure naturally goes down.
7. Garnish with sliced scallions or parsley and serve.

- Instead of soaking, the chestnuts may be dry roasted over a medium flame and the husk removed.
- The amount of chestnuts may be adjusted according to taste. Generally, a ratio of 80% rice and 20% chestnuts makes a nice balance.

CONGEE

- Beneficial for general health and for digestive problems

Congee is a traditional rice porridge eaten throughout Asia, from China and Southeast Asia to Japan. It has a soupy consistency and is much softer than ordinary rice or soft rice (see RICE PORRIDGE). For medicinal cooking, various ingredients may be added to congee.

1. Add a pinch of sea salt to 10 cups of water and bring to a boil.
2. Add 1 cup brown rice and cook over a medium to medium-high heat for about 30 minutes. If the heat is too low, the rice will sink and may burn.
3. Leave the pot uncovered or only half covered to prevent water from overflowing. Stir occasionally to prevent burning.
4. Add additional water as necessary to keep the desired consistency. The congee should be semi-solid.
5. Garnish with sliced scallions or parsley.

- For spleen troubles, add a small volume of Chinese jujubes with the rice. (These are available at Oriental markets.)

FERMENTED RICE

- Beneficial for digestion, strengthening the liver and intestines

In Asia, fermented starters made from microorganisms, bacteria, yeasts, or molds are used with rice to make a range of products including amasake, mirin, rice vinegar, sake, and many types of flat bread and cakes. The starters are known as *koji* in Japan, *chu* in China, *nuruk* in Korean, *ragi* in Southeast Asia, and *bakhar, ranu,* or *marchaar* in India. Below are several fermented rice dishes.

Idli Steamed Bread

Idli is small, white, steamed flat bread or cake popular among the Tamils of South India. It is prepared by fermenting a thick batter of thoroughly washed rice and black gram dhal, a form of curried lentils. After fermenting, the batter, or *dosa*, is steamed or fried to yield a large, thin, crispy pancake. Scientific studies have found that fermented rice helps prevent fat accumulation in the liver.

1. Soak 1 1/2 cups long grain brown rice for 6 hours and 1/2 cup black gram, washed, for 4 hours.
2. Grind the rice coarsely in a grinder and separately grind the black gram finely. Add water while grinding to make a uniform paste, but do not add too much liquid.
3. Mix the two ground ingredients with sea salt to taste, stir, and let ferment for 8 hours.
4. Idli is cooked in a special idli maker that is available at Indian or South Asian specialty shops. Otherwise, prepare like pancakes in a little sesame oil in a skillet for several minutes

Fermented Rice Drink

This mildly fermented, non-alcoholic beverage tastes like whey and is helpful for digestion and minor ailments.

1. Soak 1 cup brown rice in 2 cups water for 16 hours (24 hours in colder weather) in a container. The best temperature for soaking is 68 to 77 degrees F.
2. Strain off the soaking water, let ferment in a warm place for another 36 to 72 hours, and drink the liquid.

FRIED RICE

- Beneficial for general health and vitality; better circulation; anemia, heart failure, irregular heartbeat, varicose veins, and other cardiovascular problems; coldness and low energy

Fried rice is very strengthening and delicious. It may be made year round, once or twice a week, as part of a balanced diet. It is especially good for circulatory conditions, coldness, and weakness. Those on an oil-less or low-fat diet can water-sauté the rice with a little water instead of oil.

1. Dice 1 celery stalk, 1 onion, and 1 medium carrot.
2. Brush the skillet with a small volume of sesame oil, let it heat for up to a minute, and sauté the veggies until crisp, but not overcooked.
3. Add 2 cups of cooked brown rice on top (either boiled or pressure cooked) and several teaspoons of water.
4. Cover the skillet and cook over a low flame for 10 to 15 minutes. Do not stir, but gently poke the rice and veggies with a wooden spoon from time to time to prevent burning.
5. Add a little shoyu (natural soy sauce) to taste.
6. Cook for another 5 minutes.
7. Gently mix just before serving.

- Vary the veggies. Other tasty combinations include cabbage, carrots, and onions; fresh peas, carrots, and onions; cabbage and mushroom; daikon and daikon tops; and fresh corn kernels and diced nori.

Fried Rice Balls and Baked Rice Balls

Fried rice balls are tasty and delicious. They are especially recommended for bone and joint conditions or for travel in cold weather. After making rice balls, add a little sesame oil to a saucepan and fry the rice balls until slightly brown. Turn over and fry the other side. Season with shoyu or gomashio and eat hot.

To protect against frostbite and very cold weather, rice balls may also be wrapped with miso, especially sweet young miso, and then baked. This will prevent the miso from sticking.

GENSHIN TEA

- Beneficial for overweight, coldness, bad breath, body odor, and other expansive conditions

Genshin tea is made from brown rice that has been roasted slowly until it is very black. It is strengthening and cleansing and can be taken 2 or 3 days in a row and then occasionally as needed, but not every day. Drink the tea slowly. A ready-made variety is available at selected natural foods stores.

1. Roast 1 cup of brown rice very slowly in a dry skillet. Stir gently from time to time with a rice paddle or wooden spoon.
2. When rice is black , add to boiling water.
3. After a minute, reduce heat and simmer for several **minutes**.
4. Strain and serve.

- Variations: For better circulation, especially for coldness, add a pinch of sea salt and a few drops of ginger juice (the squeezed liquid from a small volume of grated fresh gingerroot) to the tea while simmering.
- Genshin tea may also be made with barley, millet, or other grain or a combination of grains. Adding a small amount of barley to rice will especially soothe the liver. Adding millet will benefit the pancreas, spleen, and stomach.

GINGER-SCALLION-RICE WINE COMPRESS

- Beneficial for sprains, healing broken bones, and other injuries and accidents; hardness in the liver and other organs; ingrown toenail; severe stomach pain and lack of appetite

This is a traditional compress used by martial arts masters to heal injuries during practice. It may also be used to relieve stagnation and pain in other organs. However, do not use on cancerous tumors. Altogether the treatment takes about 1 to 1 1/2 hours. Use only once or twice a week for most conditions. Many will clear up in that time.

1. Grate 1/2 cup of fresh gingerroot.
2. Finely chop 1/2 cup scallions (white part only)
3. Place ingredients in a small saucepan and add enough rice wine (sake) to cover.
4. Bring to a boil.
5. Strain off the water and put the ginger-scallion mixture into a small cheesecloth bag.
6. Apply on the affected region.
7. When the compress cools, use the hand to gently stimulate energy flow on the injured area or use the palm to supply extra energy or drain away excess energy (in case of an inflammation).
8. Repeat the process, heating the compress again, placing over the area, and sending energy with the hand.

GINGER TEA WITH RICE

- Beneficial to stimulate digestion, improve circulation, provide warmth, and help relieve nausea, motion sickness, sore throat and hoarseness, and other ailments

Ginger tea with rice is a traditional medicinal drink in China, the Philippines, and other Asian countries. A small amount is customarily taken a half hour before a journey to prevent motion sickness.

1. Boil 1 cup of water.
2. Add 1 teaspoon of roasted rice and a small piece of fresh gingerroot. See ROASTED RICE for instructions on how to prepare.
3. Boil for 1 minute.
4. Strain, let cool, and drink.

- The Chinese customarily make this tea by placing 1/2 cup of rice in a flat dish, cover with water, and soak overnight. In the morning, drain the excess liquid, roast the rice in a dry skillet, stirring constantly until parched and dark. The unused rice may be kept in a glass container for future use. Cover tightly to keep out moisture.

- Contraindication: this tea is generally not given to pregnant mothers and should be avoided by those with cancer, AIDS, or infectious conditions.

HATO-MUGI RICE

- Beneficial for general good health, for skin care and natural beauty, and to gain weight

Hato mugi, also known as *pearl barley* or *Job's tears,* yields a shiny, pearl white grain when cooked. In the East, it is customarily taken to cleanse and beautify the skin and face. It may also be steeped into a medicinal tea or used in a compress. Hato mugi's high fat content makes it a good food for those who need to gain weight. However, for cancer and other conditions where excess fat (of animal or vegetable quality) is usually not recommended, avoid until the condition improves.

Like wild rice, hato mugi is expensive and a small volume goes a long way. Cooked together with rice, it is very delicious, chewy, and attractive.

1. Wash 2 cups brown rice and $1/2$ cup of hato mugi and place in a pressure cooker.
2. Add 2 pinches of sea salt, cover, and bring up to pressure.
3. Cook for 45 to 50 minutes.
4. Let sit for 5 minutes and allow the pressure to come down naturally.
5. Gently remove from the pot and serve.

- This dish may also be boiled following the basic recipe for BOILED RICE.
- Hato mugi (pearl barley) should not be confused with *pearled barley*, a common form of polished barley. Hato mugi is available in select natural foods stores or from mail order companies.

MILLET RICE

- Beneficial for general good health; diabetes, hypoglycemia, and other pancreatic disorders; stomach problems; spleen and lymphatic problems, including infectious disease

Millet cooked with rice adds sweetness, texture, and strength to regular rice.

1. Wash 2 cups brown rice and $1/2$ cup of millet and place in a pressure cooker with 5 cups water.
2. Add a pinch of sea salt, cover, and bring up to pressure.
3. Cook for 45 to 50 minutes.
4. Let sit for 5 minutes and allow the pressure to come down naturally.
5. Gently remove from the pot and serve.

Soft Millet Rice

This porridge is very delicious and may be made fresh or prepared with leftover grain.

1. If preparing fresh, follow above recipe, using 4 to 5 cups of water per cup and a pinch of sea salt per cup of grain.
2. If using leftover grain, place in a saucepan, add about $1/3$ to $1/2$ the volume of water, and cook for 15 to 20 minutes until soft.

MOCHI

- Beneficial for general good health as well as medicinally for infertility (in men and women), underweight, lack of breast milk in nursing mothers, anemia, stress and tension, coldness, insomnia, sadness and other mental, emotional, and nervous troubles

Mochi is made from sweet rice that has been pounded and shaped into small pieces. It is traditionally enjoyed as a festive dish or prepared for special occasions. It can be made at home by pounding cooked sweet rice with a heavy wooden pestle in a wooden bowl. It is also available ready-made in natural foods stores.

Mochi may be pan-fried, steamed, baked, sautéed in oil, deep-fried, or added to soups and stews. It is enjoyed plain or served with a variety of toppings, including shoyu, barley malt, or rice syrup.

Home Made Mochi

1. Wash 2 cups of sweet brown rice and soak several hours or overnight and pressure cook following basic recipe for PRESSURE-COOKED RICE.
2. When done, pound the rice in a wooden bowl with a heavy pestle or mallet until all the grains are crushed and sticky and the texture is smooth.
3. Wet the pestle occasionally to prevent rice from sticking. Proper mochi takes about a half hour or more of pounding.
4. Form the mochi into small balls, cakes, or squares or spread in one large square or rectangular piece, about $1/2$ to 1 inch thick, on an oiled or floured baking sheet.
5. Allow to dry for 1 to 2 days.
6. Store covered in a refrigerator or keep in a cool, dry room.
7. To serve, cut into bite-sized pieces and steam, pan fry, bake, or prepare in other ways.

Pan-Fried Mochi

Mochi is commonly pan-fried on top of the stove in an oil-free skillet. For medicinal dishes, especially for those who must limit their oil intake, this is the standard method.

1. Cut the mochi into small bite-sized pieces, 1 to 2 inches square.
2. Place the pieces in a preheated, dry skillet for about 5 minutes on each side on a low to medium flame. (The skillet may or may not be covered with a lid.)
3. The cakes or squares will expand and puff up when done and may be slightly browned on the outside something like marshmallows. Check frequently or the mochi will expand and burst.
4. Serve plain or with a topping. For those who can enjoy sweets, mochi may be topped with brown rice syrup, barley malt, fruit preserves, or other sweetener. For those who are healing, a little shoyu or kinako (roasted soybean flour) may be used instead. Mochi is also very delicious wrapped in toasted nori seaweed.

Fried Mochi

Mochi fried in oil gives a rich, warming taste and energy. This style of preparation is particularly good for anemia, coldness, bone or arthritic conditions, and pregnant mothers.

1. Spread a small volume of sesame oil on the bottom of a frying pan and heat it.
2. When the oil has been spread completely, place in it some brown rice mochi, which has been cut into 1-inch squares.
3. Cover and fry until soft. Turn the mochi over, and fry for another few minutes.
4. Dip in topping and serve.

- Variation: Add the fried mochi to miso soup and cook it at the same time.
- Wrap the oil-fried mochi in narrow nori strips that have been dipped in shoyu or spicy nori strips.

Mochi in Bancha Twig Tea

This preparation is especially good for pregnancy poisoning and other complications of pregnancy. However, its soft consistency may be beneficial to others with appetite loss or difficulty swallowing.

1. Prepare pan-fried mochi as described in the above recipe.
2. Prepare bancha twig tea
3. After the mochi is very soft, place it in a rice bowl.

4. Immediately pour strained bancha twig tea over the melting mochi.

Mochi in Miso Soup

Miso, a fermented paste made with soybeans and usually barley or rice, is extremely beneficial for the intestines and strengthens all other systems and functions of the body. It is customary prepared into soup. Adding mochi to miso soup provides strength, increases energy, and strengthens the blood. This dish is particularly good for anemia, nervous conditions, circulatory problems, and other weakened conditions.

1. Cut mochi into $1/2$ inch squares.
2. Pan-fry or oil-fry following either recipe described above.
3. Prepare miso soup by soaking a small 1 to 2-inch piece of wakame dried sea vegetable for 5 minutes and cut into small pieces.
4. Add the wakame to 1 quart of fresh, cold water and bring to a boil.
5. Cut 1 cup onions, sliced thinly, into small pieces, and slice $1/2$ cup kale or other leafy green vegetable.
6. Add the vegetables to the boiling broth and boil for 3-5 minutes until soft and edible. Reduce flame to low.
7. Dilute miso (1/2 to 1 level teaspoon per cup of broth) in a little broth or fresh water, add to soup, and simmer for 3-4 minutes on a low flame.
8. Once the miso is added, don't boil the soup. Just let it simmer.
9. Garnish with finely chopped scallions or parsley before serving.
10. When the mochi is softly melted, place it in a soup bowl. Immediately pour the hot MISO SOUP over the mochi.

- For softer mochi, simmer for a few minutes in the soup.
- Uncooked mochi may be used instead of pan-fried.
- For a creamy texture, grate mochi directly into the soup.
- For healing, use a barley miso, brown rice miso, or all soybean (hatcho) miso that has aged a minimum of 2 years.
- Vary the vegetables daily, using leafy greens as much as possible.
- A small volume of shiitake mushrooms (soaked and finely chopped beforehand) may be added and cooked with the other vegetables from time to time.
- For the most beneficial effect, miso soup should be cooked fresh each time and not be reused at later meals or stored overnight.

OHAGI

- Provides a good quality sweet taste and is beneficial for hypoglycemia, diabetes, leukemia, and other conditions

Ohagis are soft, dumpling-size balls of brown rice and sweet brown rice coated or filled with sweetened aduki beans, squash, chestnuts, or other ingredients. A festive dish traditionally enjoyed in the Far East, they may be used medicinally to provide a sweet taste and complex carbohydrates to people with blood sugar problems or those who crave simple sugars.

1. Cook 2 cups of sweet rice with 3 cups of water and a pinch of sea salt, as in the recipe for PRESSURE-COOKED RICE.
2. Pound the rice in a wooden bowl with a heavy pestle or mallet until all the grains are half crushed and sticky. Wet the pestle occasionally to prevent the rice from sticking to it. Pounding takes about 20 minutes or more.
3. Form the dough into small balls and coat with toppings.
4. For ohagis coated with aduki beans, soak the aduki beans overnight, and cook them the next morning. Add a little barley malt and salt for seasoning several minutes before putting out the flame, and then mix well. Mash well with a mortar or suribachi. Cover the small rice ball with aduki paste $1/4$ inch thick when the aduki mixture has cooled.
5. For ohagis covered with squash, peel the skin of a medium size squash or pumpkin and cut it in pieces. Place in a saucepan with a lid and add water to a level of about one third the vegetable pieces. Cook over a strong flame, reduce when it starts to boil, and cook until tender. Add a pinch of salt and cook another 2 to 3 minutes. Mash it in a suribachi. When it is cool, cover the small rice ball with the paste to make it about 1/4-inch thick.
6. For ohagis covered with chestnuts, shell a cup or more of chestnuts and put them in a saucepan with a lid. Add water to a level of about one third the chestnuts. Cook with a strong flame, reduce when it starts to boil, and cook until the chestnuts become soft. Add a pinch of salt, cook another 3-4 minutes, and mash in suribachi. When the mixture has cooled, cover the small rice balls with the paste to about $1/4$ inch thick. Note that dried chestnuts must be soaked overnight.

OJIYA

- Beneficial for sleeping problems, dizziness, anemia and circulatory problems, ankylosing spondilitis, environmental illness, prostate cancer, leukemia, and other conditions

Ojiya is a soft porridge made with brown rice, sweet vegetables, root vegetables, and leafy greens, and seasoned with miso, or fermented soybean paste. Also known as *miso zosui*, it is strengthening and delicious. Take daily for several days and then occasionally as needed.

1. Boil 1 cup of brown rice in 3 cups of water.
2. Chop finely a variety of vegetables such as butternut or buttercup squash, onion, carrots, cabbage, and daikon and add to the cooked grain. Simmer until all the ingredients are soft and creamy.
3. Add a small volume of puréed miso (preferably aged at least 2 years) and stir gently. This may vary between 1 and 3 teaspoons.
4. Simmer over a low flame for another 2 to 3 minutes.
5. Remove pot from the stove and let sit for 5 minutes before serving. Add chopped scallions as a garnish.

- Variations: Ojiya may also be prepared by layering: place the vegetables in the pot, beginning with the lightest, add the grain on top, and cook together in 2 $1/2$ to 3 cups of water.
- Leftover rice may be used instead of fresh rice. Add twice as much water as rice and follow steps 2 to 5 above.
- For stomach, spleen, and pancreatic problems, add about 20% millet to 80% rice. For liver or bone conditions, add some barley.
- For anemia, coldness, or circulatory problems, add a small amount of scallion or garlic.
- Another nice combination of vegetables is cabbage, dried shiitake mushroom, daikon, daikon leaves, and onion. Pumpkin, acorn squash, and other sweet vegetables may also be used. Nori may also be added and cooked into the porridge if desired.

PRESSURE-COOKED RICE

- Beneficial for general good health, many healing conditions, strengthening the intestines, lungs, kidneys and bladder, liver, pancreas, stomach, and spleen, and creating a calm, peaceful mind and spirit

Pressure cooked brown rice is the staple in millions of macrobiotic, vegetarian, and traditional households around the world. Alternated occasionally with boiled rice, it is prepared fresh daily and used for the main meal of the day, reheated with the addition of more liquid the next morning for a breakfast porridge, and then steamed, fried, prepared into other dishes for the midday meal. As a medicinal dish, pressure-cooked rice is the central food for many conditions and disorders. Limit pressure-cooking for contractive conditions.

1. Gently wash the rice in cold water.
2. Place 2 cups of organic brown rice in a pressure cooker and smooth the surface of the grain so it is level.
3. Add $3\ 1/2$ to 4 cups of water slowly down the side of the pressure cooker so the surface of the rice remains even and calm.
4. Add 2 pinches of sea salt, cover, and bring up to pressure slowly.
5. When pressure is up, place a flame deflector underneath and turn flame to medium low, just enough to maintain pressure. (If you don't have a deflector, keep flame as low as possible.)
6. Cook for 50 minutes from the time the pressure is up.
7. When rice is done, remove the pressure cooker from the burner and let the pressure come down naturally, about 5 minutes.
8. Remove the cover, and let the rice sit for a few minutes so that it will not stick to the bottom.
9. Transfer rice to a serving bowl. If possible, use wooden implements such as a rice paddle or wooden spoon and serving bowl. Rice prepared in this way has a delicious, nutty taste and gives strong, peaceful energy.

- Soaking the rice for several hours or overnight will make it more digestible.
- Instead of salt, the rice may be seasoned with a small piece of kombu the size of a postage stamp.
- Each cup of uncooked rice yields about 3 cups of cooked rice.

Allow about 1 cup of cooked rice per person.
- Leftover rice will usually keep about 24 hours unrefrigerated in a wooden bowl covered with a thin bamboo mat or cotton towel. If it is hot or humid, keep in the refrigerator in a closed container.
- Warm up leftover rice in a small steamer or place in a small saucepan, add a little water, cover, and heat for a few minutes.
- For variety, pressure cook rice with 10-20% barley, millet, corn, or other grain. Or add 10-20% lentils, aduki beans, chickpeas, or other beans.

RAW RICE

- Beneficial for eye problems, worms and parasites

Raw rice has customarily been used to treat eye problems including inflammations, bloodshot eyes, glaucoma, and other conditions. Applying the rising energy of fire to the rice, or cooking, creates an upward energy that could further inflame the eyes. Rather, the gathering, downward energy of pounding and kneading takes pressure off the eyes. Raw rice is also traditionally used to eliminate worms from the body.

1. The rice is slightly softened first by soaking it in water for several hours.
2. Drain the water and crush the moist grains in a mortar or suribachi.
3. Add a little water and knead the mixture and pound further in the mortar.
4. Eat a small volume of the raw rice, chewing well, 50 to 100 times per mouthful.

- Without cooking, this rice will keep for 4 to 5 days.
- Eye problems correspond with the liver in Eastern medicine and philosophy. Extreme foods that tax the liver such as heavy animal food, alcohol, sugar, and toxins may also result in eye problems.
- To relieve worms, don't eat breakfast in the morning. For lunch, eat a handful of raw brown rice combined with raw seeds (such as pumpkin, sunflower, squash, or watermelon seeds) and some chopped raw scallions, onions, or garlic. Eat a regular meal at dinner. After several days, the worms will become intoxicated and begin to leave the body.

RICE BALLS

- Beneficial for general health, as a quick lunch or supper, for traveling, and medicinally for strength and vitality for a variety of conditions and emergencies such as colitis, immune disorders, miscarriage, infectious disease, blood and lymph problems, and exposure to nuclear radiation or fallout

Rice balls are invaluable for many conditions and emergencies. In Japan, people in Hiroshima and Nagasaki who ate rice balls, along with miso soup, sea vegetables, and other simple foods, survived the deadly radiation of the atomic bombs, while many others perished.

Rice balls make excellent travel food because they are easy to transport, do not require utensils, and keep fresh for one to two days or longer. They are traditionally wrapped outside with nori sea vegetable and contain umeboshi plum inside, giving the rice ball its tangy flavor and helping to preserve it without refrigeration. The standard rice ball is triangular or wedge-shaped.

1. Toast 1 sheet of nori by holding the shiny side over a burner about 10-12 inches from the flame. Rotate for 3-5 seconds until the color changes from black to green. Fold nori in half and fold again so you have four pieces that are about 3 inches square.
2. Add a pinch of salt to the dish of water and wet your hands.
3. Form a handful of previously cooked rice into a triangle by cupping your hands into a V shape.
4. With your thumb, press a hole in the center and place $1/2$ to 1 pitted umeboshi plum inside. Close hole and knead rice ball again until it is compact.
5. Cover rice ball with nori, one square at a time, until it sticks. Wet hands from time to time in salted water to prevent rice and nori from sticking to your skin, but do not use too much water.

- For variety, make round rice balls instead of triangles by forming into solid balls.
- In addition to regular rice, make rice balls with about 1/2 cup sweet brown rice to 1 1/2 cups brown rice.
- As an outside coating instead of nori, roll the rice balls in roasted crushed sesame seeds, shiso leaves, dried wakame sheets, or green leafy vegetable leaves.

RICE WITH BEANS

- Beneficial for general health, kidney and bladder problems, and ear and hearing troubles

1. Wash 2 cups of brown rice and $1/5$ to $1/4$ cup of beans.
2. Boil beans for 30 minutes in about 2 cups of water before starting the rice.
3. Allow beans to cool and then place beans in a pressure cooker along with the rice, the bean cooking water, and 2 pinches of sea salt.
4. Add extra water so that altogether there are from 4 cups of liquid in the pressure cooker (counting the bean water, which will vary slightly from bean to bean).
5. Pressure cook for 45 to 50 minutes.
6. Allow pressure to come down naturally, take off lid, and serve.

- Aduki beans are higher in protein, lower in fat and oil, and more compact than many other beans. They are traditionally considered the most strengthening bean, especially for kidney and bladder conditions. Other smaller beans, such as lentils, chickpeas, and black soybeans, are also beneficial. For medicinal use, lima and other larger beans are generally avoided. Similarly, split beans, such as split peas, are suitable for ordinary use on occasion, but generally not used for healing because their energy is dispersed in processing.

RICE BRAN COMPRESS

- Beneficial for skin inflammations, allergies, eczema, itching, and other skin conditions

Rice bran is known in the East as *nuka*. It is made from the bran or outer layer of whole grain rice that is removed to make polished white rice. Traditionally, bran was used to make pickles and soap. As an external application, it was prized for its cleansing power for the skin. It acts to soothe skin inflammation or irritation. Actually, this high-fiber component has similar internal effects, serving to cleanse and strengthen the intestines and other organs. This is a major reason why eating whole grain rice (including the bran and germ) is highly recommended. Rice bran is available in selected natural foods stores or Oriental markets.

1. Put several handfuls of rice bran in a small cotton bag or cheesecloth, and tie the bag with cotton string.
2. Bring 2 to 3 quarts of water to a boil, and drop in the rice bran, shaking the bag from time to time. The water should become milky yellow.
3. Soak the brown rice bran bag in lukewarm water and gently apply it on the affected part.

- Do not discard the water after using it for compresses. Use it instead for washing yourself or add it to a bath.
- For overall cleansing, scrub your entire body with the rice bran compress for 5-10 minutes daily.

RICE BRAN PICKLES

- Beneficial for digestion, stomach and intestinal troubles, and for strength and vitality

Rice bran pickles can be made with many ingredients and fermented from several hours and days to months and years. The most famous, Takuan pickles, are made with daikon, rice bran, and salt. They take their name from a 17th century Zen monk who introduced this method of preparation. These strong, salty pickles are customarily aged 1 to 3 years, give powerful energy and vitality, and are known as samurai pickles. The following recipe is for novice Takuan, aged 3 to 5 months.

1. Quickly dry roast 10 to 12 cups rice bran in a skillet over a medium to low flame until a nutty fragrance is released.
2. Mix roasted bran with 1 1/2 to 2 cups sea salt and cover the bottom of a pickle crock or keg with the mixture.
3. Add a layer of whole dried daikon (dried outdoors in the sun for several days).
4. Add another layer of bran and salt, alternating with the dried vegetables. Use bran for the last layer.
5. **Add 3 to 5 cups water, but the consistency should remain thick.**
6. Insert a wooden disc or plate into the crock on top of the mixture, place a heavy weight (or clean stone or jar filled with water) on top of the mixture, and let it press down on the ingredients. The plate or disk should be wide enough to cover the contents but loose enough to fit within the crock comfortably.
7. Cover with a cheesecloth or cotton cloth and place in a cool, dark place.
8. When water rises, lighten the weight.
9. When pickles are done, rinse off the bran, slice, and eat.

- Since rice bran is the byproduct of polishing white rice, brown rice flour may be substituted.
- For short-time pickling, slice daikon into smaller pieces and add only 1/8 to 1/4 cup salt. They should be done in 1 to 2 weeks.
- Other types of rice pickles include sake lees pickles (*kasu-zuke*), made from the residue of the sake making process, and *koji-zuke*, made from koji, the starter used to make amasake, miso, shoyu, and other fermented foods.

RICE BRAN PLASTER

- Beneficial for allergies, boils, broken bones, hives, infections, inflammations, poison ivy, rashes, and other skin conditions, including a red or purplish color

The rice bran plaster (known in Japanese as *nuka*) has a similar effect as the RICE BRAN COMPRESS. However, the plaster is made with flour and placed on the affected area for **typically several hours**, while the compress is used more as an immediate soothing or scrubbing agent.

Dairy products, oily, greasy foods, and flour products are primary causes of skin problems. As a rule, commercial body care products, including soaps, creams, and lotions, also clog the meridians, acupressure points, and sweat glands, further impeding ki energy flow.

Dry skin results from a layer of oil and fat blocking the skin, not from a lack of oil. Rice bran is very helpful for dry skin, oily skin, and many other skin conditions. It is soothing for broken bones and may also be put on the toes for frostbite lesions.

1. To a handful of rice bran, add about $1/3$ as much flour, and mix together. Rice flour or hato mugi flour are traditionally used. Otherwise use whole wheat flour or white flour.
2. Add cold water as needed to make a thick paste.
3. Put the mixture in a cheesecloth, dip in hot water, and apply on the skin or affected region.
4. Rinse the plaster off and apply a fresh one when it becomes warm **(usually after 15 minutes).**

- Rice bran water may be applied around the vagina, but do not use as a douche because the brany texture may irritate this region. Rice bran may also be added to the bath.
- Use wheat bran or oat bran if rice bran is not available.

RICE BREAD

- Beneficial for general health and for many healing conditions

Bread made from rice or rice flour is popular in many traditional rice growing regions. It is especially popular with those who have difficulty digesting wheat.

Rice Kayu Bread

Kayu is the Japanese word for soft rice. The following recipe was developed by George Ohsawa, the modern macrobiotic pioneer, who was seeking a healthful alternative to baked bread and other flour products that are hard on the intestines and often create excessive mucus in the body. Made with softly cooked rice and steamed rather than baked, rice kayu bread yields a wholesome, delicious loaf that is enjoyed in households, bakeries, and restaurants around the world.

1. Mix 2 cups whole wheat flour and $1/8$ to $1/4$ teaspoon sea salt together.
2. Add 2 cups softly cooked brown rice and form dough into a ball. (See basic recipe for RICE PORRIDGE to make the soft rice.)
3. Knead the dough 350 to 400 times, adding a little more flour from time to time to prevent sticking.
4. Oil an 8-inch square pan with a little sesame oil and lightly dust the pan with the flour.
5. Shape the dough into a loaf and place it in the pan, pressing down around the dges to form a rounded loaf.
6. With a sharp knife, make a shallow slit in the top center of the dough.
7. Place the loaf in a warm place, such as a warm radiator or a pilot-lit oven and let sit for 8 to 10 hours.
8. Occasionally moisten with a warm, damp towel to prevent drying.
9. After the dough has risen, steam on top of the stove for about an hour in the covered baking pan or dish.
10. When done, remove and place on a rack to cool.

- This bread may also be baked for those who can enjoy baked bread. After the dough has risen, bake in a pre-heated 250 to 300

degree oven for about 30 minutes. Increase the temperature to 350 degrees and bake for another hour and 15 minutes.
- Add mulberries, raisins, or roasted seeds or nuts into the dough for a sweeter or crunchier loaf.

Carolina Rice and Wheat Bread

In South Carolina, where enslaved Africans introduced rice cuisine, cooked rice was combined with wheat to make a tasty loaf. This recipe is Sarah Rutledge's famous cookbook, *The Carolina Housewife*, published in Charleston in 1847.

1. Simmer 1 pound of rice in 2 quarts of water until soft.
2. When cooled, mix it well with 4 pounds of whole wheat flour, 4 large spoonfuls of yeast, and salt.
3. Let it rise before the fire.
4. Some of the flour should be reserved to make the loaves.
5. If the rice swells greatly, and requires more water, add as much as you think proper.

RICE CAKES

- Beneficial for general health and as a high quality snack for those who are healing

In traditional society, rice cakes refer to an array of rice preparations fashioned into different shapes and sizes, cooked in various ways, and filled or topped with many ingredients. They are usually divided into categories by the way they are made: pounded or kneaded, pressed, steamed, or fried. In Japan, *mochi* and *ohagis* are popular forms of rice cakes, while in Korea they are called *ttok*. They may be topped or filled with chestnut pureé, aduki bean paste, sesame seed paste or wrapped with nori. Traditional rice cakes may be shaped into squares, crescents, rounds, or long, thin cylinders. Rice cakes are usually served on New Year's and other special occasions. They may also be featured in rituals and ceremonies. See MOCHI and OHAGI.

Circular rice cakes made of dried, puffed brown rice are popular in modern society. They generally may be enjoyed in moderation by those who are healing. However, they can have a drying, tightening effect and may not be recommended for people with prostate or ovarian problems or other contractive conditions. As a general rule, it is best to limit consumption to just 1 or 2 rice cakes at a time, several times a week. Good quality toppings for dried, puffed rice cakes include: tofu spread with diced carrots and celery (all lightly boiled), onion or squash butter, chestnut purée, apple butter or apple cider jam (organic, sugar-free), fruit preserves (organic, sugar-free), barley malt or rice syrup (small amount), humous (ground chickpea dip), and sesame butter or tahini (if health permits)

Sweet Rice Cakes

A Vietnamese specialty, these sweet rice cakes, known as *Banh o* or *to*, are traditionally served on Tet, the Vietnamese New Year.

1. Mix 1/3 cup sweet brown rice flour, 1 pinch powdered ginger, 2 tablespoons rice syrup, and about 1/6 cup water and make into a dough.
2. Spread it into a square about 1/2 inch thick.
3. Line a steamer with lighted oiled aluminum foil, place the dough on it, and cook for 20 minutes.
4. Enjoy the cake plain or cut into slices and fry.

Small Fried Rice Cakes

Known as *kham-fa-roush* in Arabic, small rice cakes are traditionally served as a dessert during Ramadan, the Islamic holy day. They are particularly popular with children. The following recipe is modified for a temperate climate and environment.

1. Combine $1/2$ cup brown rice flour, $1/4$ cup brown rice syrup, and a pinch of sea salt, adding a little water as necessary to make a doughlike consistency.
2. Add $1/2$ inch sesame oil to a small saucepan and heat.
3. Deep-fry rounded teaspoons of the mixture in the hot oil, turning over and browning each side.
4. Drain on a paper towel and serve warm.

- For those who can have spices, this dish is traditionally made with a $1/2$ teaspoon saffron and $1/2$ teaspoon ground cardamon. Baking powder, rose water, and vanilla may also be added.

Sweet and Savory Rice Cakes

Rice has been used in traditional Jewish cooking for many centuries. Rice cakes are sometimes eaten to break the fast after Yom Kippur. They are served with a chutney sauce and draped with salmon fillets. Vegetarians may use a wheatmeat or soy substitute.

1. Boil 1 cup sweet brown rice and let cool.
2. Sauté 2 tablespoons sweet red onion, diced, in a little sesame oil for several minutes, and let cool.
3. Soak 2 ounces raisins, currants, or mulberries in warm water for several minutes, drain, and let dry.
4. Combine the rice, onions, and fruit along with 2 tablespoons whole mustard seeds, 4 tablespoons chives (cut on a diagonal), sea salt to taste, and $1/8$ teaspoon black pepper (optional).
5. Moisten hands and fashion into rice cakes about $1/2$ inch or more thick.
6. Sauté rice cakes in a little sesame oil until brown, turning over and cooking both sides evenly.
7. Serve with a citrus or ginger sauce and, if desired, topped with broiled tempeh, seitan, or tofu.

RICE WITH CORN

- Beneficial for general health and for heart troubles, circulatory problems, and digestive and intestinal disorders

Rice cooked with corn gives a sweet, delicious flavor that is especially cooling for the summer, but may be enjoyed year round. In traditional Eastern philosophy and medicine, corn particularly nourishes the heart and small intestine.

Because of the widespread contamination of corn by genetically engineered pollen, it is essential to obtain organic corn or conventional non-GMO corn.

1. Cut the kernels from an ear of fresh corn with a knife.
2. Add $1/2$ cup of fresh corn kernels to 2 cups of brown rice.
3. Follow the recipes for PRESSURE-COOKED RICE or BOILED RICE.

- When making corn-on-the-cob, instead of butter, salt, and pepper, season at the table with a small volume of umeboshi plum or paste. It has a tart, salty flavor and will strengthen the intestines and overall digestion. But don't use too much umeboshi, just a slice from a fresh plum or a $1/2$ teaspoon of paste.

RICE CREAM

- Beneficial for general vitality and strength, to promote breast-feeding, for sick children, for many medicinal conditions and disorders such as stroke and Down syndrome, and for patients after surgery

Rice cream is especially recommended for sick persons who cannot chew, have no appetite, or cannot keep food down. It should be prepared fresh and given daily. The powdered rice cream available in the natural foods store is not recommended for regular or medicinal use. Its energy and vitality have been dispersed. Home made brown rice cream retains the strong, whole energy of the grain and is freshly prepared. It is sometimes called Genuine Rice Cream to distinguish it from the processed variety.

1. Dry-roast 1 cup of brown rice in a cast-iron or stainless steel skillet until golden brown.
2. Place in a pot, add 10 cups of water, and a pinch of sea salt or $1/2$ umeboshi plum, and bring to a boil.
3. Cover, lower heat, and place flame deflector beneath pot and turn flame to low.
4. Cook for about 2 hours until the water is about half its original volume.
5. Let the rice cool sufficiently to be handled and place in a cheesecloth or clean unbleached muslin cloth. Tie and squeeze out the creamy liquid into a pot.
6. Reheat the creamy liquid, adding a little more seasoning if needed. Garnish with scallions, chopped parsley, nori, gomashio, or sunflower seeds.

- The remaining pulp can be saved and eaten. Make into a small ball and steam with grated carrot, lotus root, or other vegetable.
- As an alternative, you may pressure cook for 1 hour instead of boiling for 2 hours.
- Rice cream may be sweetened at the end of cooking with a little brown rice syrup, barley malt, amasake, or apple juice. However, sweeteners may need to be avoided or limited for expansive, weakened conditions.

RICE CROQUETTES

- Beneficial for general health, for energy and vitality, and for many bone and joint problems

Rice croquettes are chewy and delicious and an excellent way to use leftover rice. They are strengthening and especially good for active, hardworking people; children and teens; and older people with arthritic or rheumatoid problems who need a little more oil in their cooking.

Wild Rice Croquettes with a Mushroom-Onion Sauce

The wild rice gives a wonderful, fruit flavor to these croquettes that enhances ordinary rice.

1. Combine 2 cups brown rice and $1/2$ cup wild rice and pressure-cook following the basic recipe for PRESSURE-COOKED RICE.
2. After rice cools, combine with $1/2$ grated carrot, 1 finely sliced scallion, and 2 tablespoons whole wheat pastry flour. Fashion into patties about $1/2$-inch thick.
3. Pan fry in a little sesame oil until each side is browned.
4. As a sauce, sauté 1 cup sliced mushrooms and 1 cup thinly sliced onions for 7 to 10 minutes.
5. Remove the mushrooms and onions from the skillet and add 2 tablespoons whole wheat flour, and 1 to 2 teaspoons shoyu.
6. Gradually add 2 tablespoons water to form the sauce. Heat gently over a low flame for several minutes to gravy-like consistency.
7. Return mushrooms to the skillet. Stir and heat up briefly
8. Garnish the sauce with chopped scallions.
9. Serve grated daikon (about 1 tablespoon per person) as a condiment to help digest the oil.

- Prepare other styles of croquettes in this way, e.g., rice with corn, rice with aduki beans, rice with millet. Other tasty sauces include miso-tahini, creamy tofu, and a sweet and sour sauce (see RICE VINEGAR).

RICE WITH DAIKON PICKLES

• Beneficial for body and mouth odor

Pickles help digest whole grains and other vegetable-quality foods. They are strengthening for the intestines. Cooked together with brown rice, they especially help to prevent or relieve body or mouth odor and smooth digestion.

1. Wash and soak 2 cups brown rice for several hours or overnight.
2. Place rice and 3 cups of water in a pressure cooker and add a pinch of sea salt.
3. Finely chop daikon bran pickles. The daikon should amount to about 10% of the rice or between 3 and 4 ounces.
4. Add the daikon pickles to the pressure cooker, cover, and turn the flame on high.
5. When the pressure is up, turn the heat to low and insert a flame deflector beneath the pressure-cooker. Cook for 50 minutes.
6. Remove the pressure cooker from the heat, and allow the pressure to come down naturally.
7. After about 10 minutes, when the pressure is down, take off the cover and place in a serving bowl.

RICE DRINK

- Beneficial for festive and special occasions and occasional medicinal use

There are a variety of drinks that can be made with cooked rice, fermented rice, or sprouted rice. Several are listed below. See also AMASAKE, RICE LIQUID, and RICE MILK.

Fermented Rice Drink Sweetened with Barley Malt

Sikhya, a fermented rice drink, is the most popular dessert drink in Korea. It is also used medicinally to prevent colds, warm the body, and stimulate digestion.

1. Soak several tablespoons barley malt in 1 cup water.
2. Combine the clear water from this mixture with 1 cup steamed or boiled rice.
3. Let the rice-barley malt water ferment for about 6 hours.
4. Boil the mixture, reduce heat, simmer for a few minutes, and drink $1/2$ to 1 small cup.

Sprouted Rice-Oat Milk

As an alternative to commercial grain beverages, this homemade rice-oat milk is less processed. Because it is made from raw, sprouted grains, use sparingly for special occasions, children's treats, or medicinally to relax and relieve a tight, contractive condition.

1. Obtain $1/4$ cup dry sprouting oats and $1/8$ cup brown rice (especially Lundberg Farms Wehani rice).
2. Soak for 12 hours and sprout for a day and a half. See SPROUTED RICE for details.
3. Rinse oat and rice sprouts, place in a blender with 1 cup water, and blend on medium for 30 seconds. Add another cup of water and blend on high for 30 to 45 seconds.
4. Strain the liquid through a cheesecloth, discard the pulp, and blend again.

RICE FAST

- Beneficial for balancing expansive conditions, for energy and vitality, and for spiritual development

Traditionally, brown rice has been eaten exclusively for several days for cleansing, healing, or spiritual insight. It gives strong, gathering energy, focuses the mind, and unifies the spirit. In modern times, macrobiotic educator George Ohsawa popularized the all-brown rice diet, known as Diet #7. It is intended to be followed for no more than 10 days. Following it longer can lead to an overcontractive condition, overly rapid and uncomfortable discharge of accumulated metabolic energy, and a narrow, rigid mind and spirit. Today, a modified form of rice fasting is recommended on occasion, from a single meal once a week, to a 1 to 3-day fast every few months, to a 7 to 10 day fast once a year or every few years. Michio Kushi, the macrobiotic educator, recommends that miso soup, condiments, pickles, and tea be taken in addition to brown rice and that all food be thoroughly chewed.

1. Prepare brown rice following the basic recipe for PRESSURE-COOKED RICE or BOILED RICE.
2. Serve in individual serving bowls, approximately 1 cup of cooked rice per person.
3. Chew each mouth at least 50 times and preferable 100 to 200 times or more, putting the chopsticks, fork, or spoon down after each bite. After thoroughly chewing the rice, pick up the chopsticks or other utensils and take another mouthful.
4. Eating an entire bowl of rice in this way may take 30 to 60 minutes. However, because the nutrients and energy are absorbed more gradually and efficiently than in ordinary eating, the person is usually completely satisfied with just 1 bowl of rice.
5. Along with the rice, serve miso soup with wakame sea vegetable and 1 or 2 seasonal vegetables (especially leafy greens), homemade pickles, gomashio or other condiment, and bancha twig tea.

- As a rule, avoid talking at meals while observing a rice fast.
- This simple way of eating is very powerful and may benefit many healing conditions. However, an overly tight, contractive condition may arise after several meals or several days of eating. In that case, it is better to stop the rice fast and return to an ordinary, balanced way of eating, including plenty of variety and scope in the diet.

RICE-GINGER COMPRESS

- Beneficial for relieving stagnation in the lungs or chest, coughs, colds, and flu

Ginger gives strong dispersing energy. It is traditionally used to make a ginger compress to relieve stagnation, increase circulation, and improve energy flow. However, by itself a ginger compress is usually too strong to be used directly on the lungs or chest. (It is commonly used on the kidneys, intestines, back, shoulders, and other less sensitive regions.) Consisting of 50% cooked rice, which gives strong centering energy, this mild, soothing compress will help open the lungs or other congested region. It is also very fragrant. This compress is popular in China and Southeast Asia.

1. Mash $1/2$ cup pressure-cooked brown rice in a mortar or suribachi until it forms a paste.
2. Grate an equal volume of fresh gingerroot and mix it thoroughly with the rice.
3. Place the compress on the affected region and cover with a cotton cloth or light towel. Leave on for up to several hours and repeat, if necessary.

- As a variation, the compress may be made by roasting brown rice in a pan and adding a few slices of raw gingerroot. Wrap the rice and ginger mixture in a cheesecloth or other cotton cloth and apply it on the chest. Leave on for up to several hours and repeat, if necessary.

RICE GOMOKU

- Beneficial for general health and vitality, better circulation, and improved energy flow

Gomoku, or five-variety rice, is a festive dish made with five or more ingredients. It is customarily served in Japan over the winter holidays or other special occasions. Traditionally made with small clams, a vegetarian gomoku may be prepared using only plant quality foods as in the following recipe.

1. Dry-roast 2 cups brown rice in a skillet, stirring gently about 10 to 15 minutes over a low heat.
2. Soak the veggies separately in warm water in small bowls: 2 tablespoons of dried lotus root for 30 minutes; 2 pieces of dried tofu for 10 minutes; 6 medium shiitake mushrooms for 10 minutes; 2 tablespoons of dried daikon for 5 minutes; and 2 1-inch squares of kombu for 5 minutes.
3. Dice the veggies, but do not mince. After soaking and cutting, you should have approximately $1/3$ cup each of lotus root, tofu, mushrooms, daikon, and kombu.
4. Place dry-roasted rice in a pressure cooker. Add all the other ingredients and mix well, including 1 teaspoon finely minced scallion roots, 1 large diced carrot, $1/3$ cup chopped seitan, and 3 cups of water. Mix well.
5. Note that because seitan contains shoyu, additional seasoning is not needed in this recipe. (If you do not use the seitan, add a pinch of sea salt.)
6. Pressure-cook for 45 to 50 minutes.
7. Remove the pressure-cooker from the burner and let sit 5 minutes or longer. Let the pressure reduce naturally, and remove the cover.
8. Garnish with scallion or parsley and serve.

- This dish may also be made with unroasted rice. Soak rice before cooking and use $1 1/2$ cups of soaking water or spring water per cup of uncooked rice.

RICE JUICE

- Beneficial for problems with the bones and joints and the kidneys and bladder

Rice juice is the liquid that rises to the surface after cooking brown rice. It is especially good for arthritis, rheumatism, and other bone and joint problems, as well as kidney or bladder infections and other urinary tract problems.

See the recipes for BOILED RICE and PRESSURE-COOKED RICE for instructions on how to make basic rice. Since cooking regular rice usually yields only a small amount of rice juice, slightly more water may be added to rice in cooking to produce more liquid at the end. For example, instead of 2 cups of water to 1 cup of uncooked rice, use $2\ 1/2$ or even 3 cups. For a related remedy, with a slightly more diluted consistency, see RICE LIQUID.

- Rice Juice from freshly cooked rice is very different from commercial rice milk sold in natural food stores. Packaged rice milk is highly processed and often highly seasoned. It is suitable for people in good health on special occasions, but not for medicinal use.

RICE LIQUID

- Beneficial for hard labor, nursing babies, Down syndrome, prostate cancer, bone and joint disorders, kidney and bladder problems

The heavy fluid that rises to the top of Rice Porridge is called Rice Liquid. In Japan, it is known as *Omoyu*. Without seasoning, it is especially good for nursing babies. For babies that have weaned and older children and adults, a small amount of sea salt may be added.

1. Wash 1 cup of brown rice, and add 10 cups of water.
2. Cook with a small pinch of sea salt, unless it is intended for a very young baby in which case no seasoning is used.
3. Follow the basic remedy for BOILED RICE, but because so much liquid is used not all of the water will be absorbed. The rice should be creamy and some of the grains should still be visible after cooking.
4. If the water boils over during cooking, turn off the heat and let the rice cool off. Then turn on the heat again and continue to cook until done.
5. Spoon off the heavy liquid that rises to the top with a wooden spoon.

- For variety, slightly stronger energy, or convenience, Rice Liquid may be pressure-cooked, using 1 cup of brown rice to 5 cups of water. Season with a small pinch of sea salt or do not season if cooking for a small infant. Follow the basic recipe for PRESSURE-COOKED RICE.
- For babies who are weaned of nursing, RICE PORRIDGE WITH BANCHA TEA is preferable to Rice Liquid. However, Rice Liquid may be given if it is cooked with a small amount of bancha twig tea. Be careful not to give black or green tea.
- In the event of hard labor, a little barley malt or brown rice syrup may be added to Rice Liquid and given to the mother.
- For prostate cancer, prepare Rice Liquid with 1 tablespoon of grated daikon, 1 chopped umeboshi plum (pitted), and chopped red shiso leaves.

RICE WITH LOTUS SEEDS

- Beneficial for usual good health and for many lung and respiratory conditions

The lotus flower is a symbol of purity and enlightenment. The root of this plant has traditionally been used as a root vegetable and for healing. The long, thin chambers of the lotus root correspond with the lungs and are excellent for strengthening the respiratory system and discharging excess mucus from the body. Lotus root tea may be prepared fresh, dried, or powdered. Lotus seeds from this same plant are about the size of chickpeas, white, and mildly crunchy. They give a unique flavor and texture to brown rice. Lotus seeds are often hard to find but may be obtained in select natural foods stores, Oriental markets, and by mail order.

1. Soak 1/2 cup lotus seeds for 3 to 4 hours.
2. Combine lotus seeds with 1 cup brown rice, 2 cups water, and pinch of sea salt in a pressure cooker.
3. Follow the basic recipe for PRESSURE-COOKED RICE.
4. Garnish with sliced scallions or parsley.

Rice Soup with Lotus Seeds

This creamy soup, a Vietnamese specialty, is especially good for babies that have just been weaned. It is also enjoyed by older children and adults of all ages.

1. Soak 1/4 cup lotus seeds for several hours, remove the skin, and take out the tiny green kernel in the middle of the lotus seeds with a toothpick.
2. Wash 1 cup brown rice, place with the lotus seeds in a pan, and add 8 cups water.
3. Bring to a boil for 10 minutes, reduce heat to low, and simmer for 1 hour or more.
4. After soup is cooked, stir gently, and serve.

- The Vietnamese customarily add a pinch of sea salt or a small volume of shoyu toward the end of cooking. For babies, little or no seasoning may be used.

RICE WITH MARINATED DRIED DAIKON

• Beneficial for skin conditions, including skin cancer

Daikon facilitates discharge of fat, oil, and other excessive nutrients and is used in many medicinal dishes and drinks. However, fresh daikon is very expansive, and for relieving expansive conditions, such as most skin problems, dried daikon produces a more balanced effect. Cooking it together with brown rice further contributes to overall harmony and stability.

1. Cut several tablespoons of dried shredded daikon very finely.
2. Marinate the chopped daikon in a mixture of 1 part shoyu and 2 parts water for 1 hour
3. Pressure cook the marinated dried daikon together with brown rice until soft. See the recipe for PRESSURE-COOKED RICE. The amount of dried daikon should be 5 to 10% of the volume of the brown rice.

RICE MILK

- Beneficial for bone and joint problems, nursing infants, and childhood conditions such as Down syndrome

Rice milk has traditionally been fed to babies, infants, and children, as well as those for whom a wholesome, high quality liquid source of nutrients is advisable. Home-made rice milk gives a calm, gentle energy, unlike commercial rice milks that are usually highly processed and may contain high amounts of sodium and other seasonings.

1. In a large pot, combine the following ingredients in the indicated proportions: 1 cup brown rice, $1/3$ cup sweet brown rice, $1/5$ cup other grain such as barley, oats, wheat, or millet, $1/5$ cup beans such as aduki beans, soybeans, or other beans, $1/5$ cup vegetables (several finely chopped vegetables, especially sweet vegetables with a minor portion or root and leafy green vegetables), $1/10$ cup sea vegetables such as kombu, nori, and wakame. Add a little sesame, olive, or other vegetable oil.
2. To this mixture, add 5 to 7 times the total amount of water. Bring to a boil, and simmer on a low flame for a long time. When all the ingredients have become very soft, turn off the heat, and let the mixture cool to a moderate temperature.
3. Place the mixture into a cheesecloth bag, tie it, and squeeze the cream out of the pulp. Some water may need to be added to the cream to make a milk-like fluid.
4. Sweeten the rice milk with rice syrup, barley malt, amasake, or apple juice until it has the same sweetness as mother's milk.
5. Put this liquid into a bottle and feed the baby.

- Vary the type of additional grains, beans, vegetables, and sea vegetables frequently.
- The ratio of grains, beans, and vegetables may be varied, but the proportion of total grain should be 60% or more.

RICE MISO PLASTER

- Beneficial as an external application to reduce inflammation, swelling, or itching; to soothe cuts and wounds

Miso has strong natural antibiotic problems and is useful for many skin problems, accidents, and emergencies. It can often by itself calm down inflammatory processes. The rice, however, gives strong gathering energy that stabilizes the healing process. Generally, select a miso that has aged a minimum of two years for the strongest healing effect. These include brown rice miso, barley miso, and all soybean (hatcho) miso.

1. Cook brown rice following basic recipe for BOILED RICE and let it cool.
2. Mash about 1 cup of rice into a paste in a suribachi or mortar.
3. Add an equal volume of miso and thoroughly mix the two together.

- Miso alone can be applied externally for bleeding, cuts and wounds, itchy skin diseases, or any kind of swelling. Just place a small dab on the affected area.

Raw Rice Plaster

This plaster may be used for wounds and other inflammations, especially if miso is not available.

1. Crush 1 cup of whole raw rice with a mortar and pestle.
2. Add a small volume of water.
3. Apply this directly to the painful area.
4. Cover with cotton and hold or tie in place.

RICE NOODLES

- Beneficial for general health and suitable for most healing conditions

Noodles made with brown rice flour have a slightly nutty taste and grainy texture. *Bifun* is a delicate, thin noodle made with rice flour and potato starch. It is light and a nice alternative to soba, udon, somen, or spaghetti, but the potato starch is not recommended for most healing conditions. Fresh home-made noodles made with brown rice flour are most ideal for medicinal use, though packaged brown rice noodles are available in select natural foods stores.

Rice Noodles in Broth

1. Bring 1 quart or more water to a boil.
2. Add 8 ounces of brown rice noodles and lower heat to medium.
3. When water boils up, add a small volume of cold water.
4. Repeat this process, known as shocking, 1 or 2 more times until noodles are done, about 8 to 10 minutes, depending on thickness.
5. To make the broth, place a 1 to 2-inch piece of kombu in a saucepan and add 4 cups fresh water.
6. Soak 2 dried shiitake mushrooms, remove their stems, and slice.
7. Add the mushrooms to the broth, bring to a boil, lower the heat, and simmer for 3 to 5 minutes.
8. Place the cooked noodles in the broth to warm up, but do not boil.
9. When hot, remove the noodles and serve immediately with some of the broth.
10. Garnish with scallions, chives, or toasted nori.

- The kombu and shiitake may be left in the broth, if desired, or eaten.
- Other ingredients that go well with noodles include carrots and onions, dried daikon, cabbage, and cooked seitan, tofu, tempeh, or fu.
- Add a little fresh grated gingerroot to the broth or on top of the noodles when serving to provide additional warmth and improve circulation.

RICE PACK

- Beneficial for shoulder and neck aches, sore knees and ankles, bone and joint problems, inflammations, headaches, and for pregnant mothers during labor

As an external remedy, a rice pack provides quick, soothing heat and relief to painful areas of the body. It is helpful for arthritis, rheumatism, muscle ache, and the aches and pains of pregnancy.

1. Place $1 \frac{1}{2}$ to 2 pounds of uncooked rice (brown or white) in a linen or cheesecloth pouch about 6 x 18 inches and place in a hot oven.
2. Heat up for several minutes until the rice is warm and gentle to the touch, but not burning.
3. Place on the affected area, cover with a cotton cloth or towel, and hold in place.
4. The pack will hold the heat for 30 to 50 minutes. Reheat, if necessary. The pack may be used indefinitely.

- A popular way to make a rice pack is to fill a long white sock with the rice and tie or sew the open end before heating. The sock flexibly adapts to many body regions, providing immediate relief. Do not overfill with rice or it will be too hard.
- Sew small loops of elastic at the ends of the sock or pack so it can be held easily in place. A cotton tie or belt may also be used to hold the pack in place.
- A rice pack may also be placed in the freezer to make a cool application for fevers and other inflammations.

RICE PORRIDGE

- Beneficial for usual good health and many medicinal conditions and disorders, including colds, flus, fever, children's ailments morning sickness and other pregnancy problems, digestive troubles, and recovery from accidents, operations, and other emergencies

Rice porridge is the principal breakfast dish in many families around the world. As a medicinal dish, it is used for general strength and vitality, to stimulate the appetite, to regulate digestion, and generally assist the recovery process. In the East, soft porridge is known as *kayu* or as *thick rice*. A more diluted porridge is known as CONGEE. In the West, rice porridge was traditionally known as *rice gruel*. Today, particularly in macrobiotic households, it is simply called *soft rice*. By whatever name, it is creamy and delicious, nourishing and restorative.

Soft Rice (Fresh Rice Porridge)

For medicinal use, soft rice ideally should be made fresh each morning.

1. Wash 1 cup of brown rice and add 8 to 10 cups of water.
2. Add a small pinch of sea salt and follow the basic method of preparing rice in the recipe for BOILED RICE
3. The rice should be creamy, though all the water may not be absorbed. After cooking, some of the grains will still be visible. In the event the water boils over while cooking, turn off the flame and allow the rice to cool off. Then turn the flame on again and continue to cook until done.
4. The heavy liquid that rises to the top of the is called RICE LIQUID or *omoyu*. It is especially good for babies or for those with bone or joint problems.

- Rice porridge may also be pressure-cooked. Use 1 cup of brown rice to 5 cups of water with a small pinch of sea salt. Follow the basic recipe for PRESSURE-COOKED RICE.
- For pregnancy problems, use a small amount of umeboshi plum to season this dish in cooking instead of salt, or serve with umeboshi plum as a condiment.

- For tight, contracting conditions or those in good health, this dish may occasionally be lightly sweetened with amasake, brown rice syrup, or barley malt. For Sunday brunch or other festive occasions, cook with dried fruit such as apricots or apples, or add as a topping.

Porridge from Leftover Rice

For ordinary use, rice left over from the day before may be reheated and made into morning porridge.

1. Place 2 cups of leftover rice in a saucepan and add 4 to 6 cups of water.
2. Bring to a gentle boil, cover, and cook until the rice has the consistency of soft porridge, about 10 to 20 minutes.
3. Garnish with gomashio sesame seed salt, chopped scallion, toasted, crumpled nori strips, umeboshi plum or paste, or other condiment.

- For variety, add several finely sliced vegetables to the rice and prepare as above.

Miso Rice Porridge

For a more strongly flavored porridge, season with a little miso ($1/2$ teaspoon per cup of porridge). Toward the end of cooking the soft porridge, dilute the miso in a small volume of water and add to the mixture. Avoid adding too much miso, or the porridge will taste salty. This is especially good for relieving digestive problems; colds, flus, and fever; and for children who have taken to many snacks, drinks, or desserts the day before.

Rice Porridge with Aduki Beans

The heavy liquid that arises from the top of this dish is traditionally known in the East as *omoyu*. It is especially good for deformed infants, breastfeeding mothers, and pregnancy poisoning.

1. Soak 1/2 cup of aduki beans for 4 hours or overnight.
2. Combine beans with 2 cups of brown rice and 5 cups of water.
3. Bring to a boil, reduce the flame to medium-low, insert a flame deflector under the pot, and simmer for 50 to 60 minutes until soft.
4. Skim off the heavy liquid and use as noted below.

- For deformity, give 1 tablespoon of the heavy liquid every day. This will help prevent the muscles from cramps and stiffness. The mother may also eat 1/2 to 1 small cup of this porridge every other day.
- Nursing mothers may eat this porridge several times a week with gomashio, umeboshi plum, or other condiment.
- After weaning, the infant may be fed soft brown rice with aduki beans. See ADUKI BEAN RICE, but prepare with more liquid.
- For pregnancy poisoning, especially pregnancy kidney, prepare the porridge without seasoning.

Rice Porridge with Bancha Tea

Soft rice made with bancha twig tea is traditionally known as *chagayu*. It is good for helping to eliminate body and mouth odor, morning sickness and other pregnancy problems, stiff shoulders, and other conditions and disorders. It may also be prepared for a baby that has weaned. However, be careful to use bancha twig tea, not green tea, black tea, or other leaf tea (all of which have caffeine).

1. Follow the recipe for basic porridge, substituting bancha twig tea for water.
2. Serve with gomashio, toasted nori, or umeboshi plum.

- For morning sickness, ectopic pregnancy, and related complications, consume this dish with umeboshi plum which provides a nice sour taste.

Rice Porridge with Barley

This dish is good for liver and gallbladder conditions.

1. Combine 50% rice and 50% barley.
2. Soak several hours or overnight for better digestibility.
3. Prepare according to the basic porridge recipe.

- For a stronger medicinal effect, especially to help eliminate excessive fat and oil in the liver or gallbladder, take 1 cup of this porridge and place in a pot with 1 tablespoon of fresh grated daikon. Bring to a boil and simmer for several minutes.

Rice Porridge with Corn

This dish is helpful for heart and circulatory problems, intestinal problems, and prostate or ovarian problems.

1. Combine 50% rice and 50% fresh corn removed from the cob.
2. Soak several hours or overnight for better digestibility.
3. Prepare according to the basic porridge recipe.

- For a lighter dish, cook the rice first or start with leftover rice, then add the corn, and simmer for another 5 minutes until the corn is soft and sweet.

Rice Porridge with Grated Daikon

This is good to help reduce the accumulation of fat and oil in and around tight, compact organs. It is especially good for tight, hardened tumors.

1. Prepare basic rice porridge, seasoned lightly with sea salt or miso.
2. Add 20 to 30% fresh grated daikon to the cooked porridge, simmer for 2 to 3 minutes, and serve.

- For ovarian tumors, add a few drops of squeezed lemon juice and mix in well with the rice-daikon porridge.
- For colon tumors, add a chopped umeboshi plum (pitted) to the rice-daikon porridge and simmer for several minutes before serving.

Rice Porridge with Grated Lotus Root

This dish is helpful for lung problems ranging from simple congestion to tumors.

1. Prepare basic rice porridge with slightly more water than usual.
2. Add 20 to 30% grated fresh lotus root and stir into the porridge.
3. Simmer on a low flame for 2 to 3 minutes.

Rice Porridge with Millet

This dish is helpful for diabetes, hypoglycemia, and other pancreatic problems, stomach problems, and spleen and lymphatic conditions.

1. Combine 75% rice and 25% millet.
2. Prepare according to the basic porridge recipe.

- For an even sweeter dish, add small pieces of butternut, buttercup, acorn, or other fall- or winter-season squash.

Rice Porridge with Millet, Buckwheat, and Vegetables

This dish is helpful for lymphatic conditions, including lymphoma.

1. Combine 1 $1/2$ cups of lightly roasted brown rice, $2/3$ cup of light roasted millet, $1/3$ cup of buckwheat groats, 1 $1/2$ cups of chopped vegetables such as carrot, daikon, onion, cabbage, or burdock, a small 1-inch square of kombu, and 5 to 7 times as much water.
2. Prepare following the basic porridge recipe.

Roasted Rice Porridge

This dish gives slightly more energy and vitality and is good for the medicinal conditions noted below.

1. Wash 1 cup brown rice and light roast in a dry skillet without oil.
2. Prepare porridge by adding 3 to 4 cups of water and boiling or pressure-cooking.

- For bone and joint problems, including rheumatoid arthritis, serve with umeboshi, shiso leaf powder, or gomashio and take several times a week.
- For uterine cancer and other tumors caused by the build up of fat and oil, add 1 tablespoon grated daikon after the porridge has cooked up, season with a little shoyu to taste, and simmer for 2 to 3 minutes.

Sweet Rice Porridge

This dish is good to help relieve insomnia and to relax.

1. Prepare following the recipe for basic RICE PORRIDGE but use sweet brown rice instead of brown rice.
2. Less water is needed than with regular rice. If pressure-cooking, use about 4 cups of water for 1 cup of rice or if boiling about 8 cups of water for 1 cup of rice.

RICE POWDER

- Beneficial for burns, scalds, inflammations, and other conditions

Rice powder refers to rice flour that is ground very finely and applied externally on an affected region. It has a cooling, soothing effect and traditionally is used in South Asia for smallpox, measles, prickly heat, and other inflammatory conditions. It reduces burning and irritation.

1. Take a handful of brown rice flour and dust thickly on the surface of the affected area.
2. Leave on until the pain and heat are allayed.
3. Repeat , if necessary, with more powder.

- If brown rice flour is not available, use white rice flour.

RICE POULTICE

- Beneficial for natural skin and beauty care, burns, scalds, erysipelas, and other conditions

Rice poultices may be made with cooked rice or fine rice flour for a variety of conditions.

Rice Flour Poultice

This poultice is traditionally put on the skin, breasts, or other area to reduce inflammation. It may also be used on burns.

1. Mill freshly cooked brown rice into powder in a handmill or use store-bought brown rice flour.
2. Add water to 1 cup of rice flour and fashion into a poultice.
3. Place on the affected region, cover with a cotton cloth, tie loosely with a strip of cotton, and leave on for 30 to 60 minutes.
4. Replace, if necessary, with another poultice.

Skin and Beauty Poultice

This poultice, based on a traditional Ayurvedic remedy from India, is beneficial for the skin and will help prevent wrinkling.

1. Place 1 to 2 cups of boiled brown rice in the center of a piece of cheesecloth or linen.
2. Tie the four corners together to make a poultice.
3. Add 1/4 cup of orange peel to 1/4 cup of sesame oil and simmer for several minutes.
4. Dip the rice poultice in the warm oil and apply to the entire body, beginning with the feet and working up the legs, midsection, arms, chest, and face and neck.
5. The entire treatment takes about 20 to 30 minutes.

RICE PUDDING

- Beneficial for ordinary or medicinal use

Rice pudding made with brown rice and other high quality ingredients is an excellent dessert for those in usual good health as well as for those recovering from illness. It is tasty, sweet, delicious, and has a mild, smooth consistency that is easy to digest. It is especially beneficial as a special treat for those who need to avoid hard baked flour products such as cakes, pies, and pastries.

1. Cook 2 cups of long-grain brown rice following the recipe for BOILED RICE or PRESSURE-COOKED RICE.
2. Place the rice, 2 tablespoons of raisins, currants, or other dried fruit, and a pinch of sea salt in a saucepan.
3. Add 3/4 cup apple juice, 3/4 cup water, and 2 tablespoons brown rice syrup.
4. Cook over a low flame for 25 minutes.
5. Dissolve 1 tablespoon kuzu in cold water and add to the other ingredients and stir in so it will thicken the mixture.
6. Serve in individual dishes and let sit until ready to serve.
7. Garnish with roasted, slivered almonds or walnuts.

- A rich, spicy rice pudding may be made by adding 1/2 teaspoon tahini and a pinch of cinnamon or nutmeg.

Amasake Pudding

This delicious, creamy dessert, made from fermented sweet rice, can be enjoyed by both those in good health and in recovery.

1. Pour 1 quart of amasake into a saucepan.
2. Dissolve 3 rounded tablespoons kuzu in a little cold water and stir into the amasake.
3. Add a pinch of sea salt and stir with a constant, gentle motion while bringing the mixture to a boil over low heat.
4. Simmer several minutes more.
5. Pour into individual serving dishes and garnish with slivered almonds.

RICE SOUP

- Beneficial for general health and for energy, vitality, warmth and many medicinal conditions

Rice soup can be made in many ways. It is an especially good way to use leftover rice. It is very nourishing, digestible, and easy to assimilate.

Brown Rice Soup

1. Boil 3 shiitake mushrooms and a small 1-inch piece kombu in 1 quart of water for 2 to 3 minutes.
2. Remove and cut into thin strips or pieces.
3. Return vegetables to the water, add 2 cups cooked brown rice, and bring to a boil.
4. Lower the heat and cook for 30 to 40 minutes.
5. Add 1/4 cup chopped celery and simmer for 5 minutes.
6. Add shoyu or miso (diluted in a little of the broth) to taste and simmer for another 5 minutes.
7. Garnish with sliced scallions and serve.

Thunder Tea Soup

This Malaysian soup (known as *lui char fan*) takes its name from the grinding of ingredients used in its preparation. It is made from a rice dish of the same name and served with several side dishes. Women traditionally grind the ingredients with a wooden pestle in a large bowl made from a guava tree trunk. The soup has a greenish color because of the various leaves that are used. Its slightly bitter taste is good for relieving flatulence. The ingredients in this dish have been adjusted slightly for a temperate climate and environment. Also the Malaysians customarily add shrimp. This is a vegan variation.

1. Grind equal amounts of several or all of the following: groundnuts, sesame seeds, peppercorns, green tea leaves, mint leaves, and sweet potato leaves.
2. Pour hot water into the grinding bowl and mix the ingredients well.

3. Place the soup in a saucepan and bring to a boil.
4. As side dishes, prepare several or all of the following: stir-fried leeks with deep-fried tofu or tempeh; stir-fried string beans; stir-fried daikon radish pickle (soaked and sliced); stir-fried lotus root; alfalfa sprouts; baked groundnuts (first toasted in the oven and then their skins removed after cooling); and pan-fried mochi.
5. To serve, take a small bowl of cooked brown rice, invert into a larger individual bowl (e.g., a noodle bowl), and add small servings from the side dishes onto the rice.
6. Pour the hot soup over the rice, mix gently with chopsticks or a spoon, and enjoy.

- The Malaysians customarily use *koo let sim* leaves, Chinese tea leaves, *ikan bilis*, and other native ingredients. As tropical substances, their energy may be too expansive for a temperate climate and stress the liver and heart.

RICE AND SWEET VEGETABLES WITH VINEGAR

- Beneficial for morning sickness

This dish is very tasty and satisfying and will be helpful to pregnant mothers with morning sickness. The vinegar and citrus provide a good quality sour taste that is often craved during pregnancy.

1. Cook 2 cups of short-grain brown rice following the basic recipe for BOILED RICE OR PRESSURE-COOKED RICE using slightly more water than usual to make the rice somewhat softer.
2. Finely slice several sweet vegetables such as carrots, butternut or buttercup squash, pumpkin, cabbage, onion, and daikon.
3. Water-sauté the vegetables with a little water in a skillet.
4. Combine the vegetables with the rice and mix well.
5. Season moderately with shoyu and umeboshi vinegar or brown rice vinegar.
6. Squeeze a few drops of fresh lemon or tangerine, if desired, for a further sour taste.

RICE SYRUP

- Beneficial for ordinary and many medicinal uses

Brown rice syrup is a thick grain-based natural sweetener resembling honey. It breaks down into complex carbohydrates that enter the digestive system more slowly and gradually than fruit, sugar, high fructose corn syrup, honey, or other sweeteners. In cooking, it is used to sweeten special dishes or sauces and to make many snacks and desserts.

Rice syrup is helpful to relax an overly stressful or tense condition, to offset tight, contractive disorders (e.g., a dry cough), and to prevent overweight or obesity. See AME KUZU TEA. Medicinally, brown rice syrup has a more downward energy than *barley malt* or *rice malt* (which is made with cooked rice and sprouted barley). Hence, for colds, fever, inflammation, and other more expansive conditions, rice syrup is preferable, since it will help bring the energy in the body down. For kidney, bladder, reproductive, bone, and other more tight, contractive conditions, the rising, upward energy of barley malt is generally better. However, barley malt tends to harden in the body more than rice syrup and can lead to stagnation, so use only in moderation.

1. As a concentrated sweetener, use only a small amount (usually from 1 teaspoon to 1 tablespoon) of rice syrup for most snacks or drinks.
2. Spread plain on mochi, arepas, rice cakes, or other snack.
3. For teas, mix a teaspoon of rice syrup in hot water and warm up for a few minutes.

- As a topping for pancakes, waffles, or pan-fried mochi, rice syrup may be diluted with a little water (and fresh strawberries, blueberries, or other fruit, if desired) and heated for several minutes in a saucepan.

RICE TEA

- Beneficial for ordinary and medicinal use

Like other grains, brown rice may be used to make a soothing, nourishing tea that is suitable for children as well as adults. Below are recipes for basic roasted rice tea and several medicinal teas that are made from cooking rice with other ingredients.

- The medicinal teas may be kept in a thermos or refrigerator and used several times. However, ideally they are made fresh every day or every other day for the strongest healing effect.
- The leftover rice and other ingredients in the medicinal teas may be eaten separately or saved for use in soups, stews, or other dishes.

Roasted Rice Tea

1. Dry-roast 1 cup of uncooked brown rice in a skillet over a medium flame for about 10 minutes or until a fragrant aroma is released.
2. Stir and shake pan occasionally to prevent burning.
3. Add 2 to 3 tablespoons of roasted rice to $1\ 1/2$ quarts of water. Bring to a boil, reduce flame, and simmer for 10-15 minutes.

Rice Tea with Aduki Beans, Dried Daikon and Shiitake

This tea is helpful for rheumatoid arthritis and kidney ailments.

1. Mix 1 cup aduki beans, 1 cup brown rice, 1 cup chopped shredded dried daikon, and 1/2 cup chopped dried shiitake mushroom.
2. Add 3 to 4 times the total volume of water.
3. Bring to a boil, reduce flame, and simmer for one-half hour.
4. Strain the liquid from the other ingredients and serve.

Rice Tea with Dried Daikon, Daikon Leaves, and Shiitake

This tea is helpful for digestive and intestinal problems, including colorectal cancer.

1. Combine 1/2 cup dried shredded daikon, 1/1 cup daikon leaves, 1/3 cup roasted brown rice, and 1/4 cup dried shiitake mushroom.
2. Add 5 cups water, bring to a boil, and simmer on a low flame for 20 to 25 minutes.
3. Strain the liquid and serve.

Rice Tea with Dried Daikon, Dried Daikon Leaves, Shiitake, and Dried Lotus Root

This tea is helpful for bladder conditions, including tumors, to help eliminate fat, oil, and other excess from the body.

1. Soak 1 cup dried daikon, 1 cup dried daikon leaves, 1/2 cup dried shiitake mushroom, and 1/2 cup dried lotus root.
2. Slice all ingredients finely.
3. Add 1 cup lightly roasted brown rice.
4. Add 3 times the total volume of water, bring to a boil, and simmer for about 25 to 30 minutes.
5. Strain the ingredients and serve.

Rice Tea with Dried Daikon, Kombu, and Shiitake

This tea is helpful for eliminating mouth and body odor.

1. Soak 1 cup dried, shredded daikon, $1/3$ cup kombu, and $1/3$ cup dried shiitake mushroom.
2. Finely chop the vegetables and place in a saucepan.
3. Add $2/3$ cup roasted brown rice and 7 cups water
4. Bring to a boil, lower the flame, and simmer for 20 to 25 minutes.
5. Strain the liquid.

Rice Tea with Dried Daikon, Shiitake, and Cabbage

This tea is helpful for brain disorders, including swelling and tumors.

1. Soak 1 cup dried shredded daikon and $1/3$ cup dried shiitake mushroom.
2. Combine with $2/3$ cup burdock or carrot and $2/3$ cup roasted brown rice.
3. Add 8 cups water, bring to a boil, and simmer for about 25 minutes.
4. Strain the liquid and serve.

Rice Tea with Lotus Root

This tea is beneficial for bronchitis, sinusitis, and other respiratory conditions. The lotus root will help discharge mucus from clogged passageways.

1. Soak $1/2$ cup dried lotus root.
2. Combine with 1 cup lightly roasted brown rice.
4. Add $4\ 1/2$ cups of water, bring to a boil, and simmer for about 25 to 30 minutes.
5. Strain the ingredients and serve.

Rice with Green Tea

Green tea is very calming and soothing, especially for tight, contractive conditions such as prostate and ovarian troubles. Prepared with brown rice, it is known as *genmai-cha*. It is commonly available in tea bags in the natural food store or may be made by preparing basic ROASTED RICE TEA above and seeping with a few pinches of green tea, straining, and serving.

- Green tea is high in antioxidants and other healthful components. But it also contains caffeine and is not recommended for many conditions, babies, or children.

RICE VINEGAR

- Beneficial for general health, digestion, circulation, and liver and gallbladder problems

Rice vinegar is a product made from brown rice or sweet brown rice and a fermented starter such as koji. It is high in acetic acid, protein, and carbohydrates and like other fermented foods, its enzymes are beneficial for digestion. The sour taste of rice vinegar especially stimulates the liver and gallbladder and can help relieve stagnation in those organs. Rice vinegar may be used to make sauces and dressings, prepare sushi, season couscous, bulghur, or other grain salads, and make pickles. Though not ordinarily used in seasoning vegetables, a touch may be added to burdock or sea vegetables to soften.

The principal types of rice vinegar are brown rice vinegar and sweet brown rice vinegar. The latter, made from sweet rice with a higher gluten content, gives a slightly sweeter taste and flavor.

Sweet and Sour Sauce

This delicious sauce may be used on brown rice, millet, noodles, tempeh, baked onions, and other dishes. The sweetness of the vegetables and apple juice will nourish the spleen and pancreas, stabilizing blood sugar levels, while the sour taste of the vinegar will stimulate the liver.

1. Prepare $1/2$ cup finely minced onion, $1/2$ cup grated carrots, and $1/2$ cup thinly sliced celery.
2. Cook the vegetables in 1 cup of dashi soup stock (made from cooking a small piece of kombu in water for 5 to 10 minutes) with a pinch of sea salt until soft.
3. When the vegetables are done, add 1 to 2 tablespoons kuzu diluted in a little cold water and stir for about 1 to 2 minutes to prevent lumping.
4. When the kuzu is thick and transparent, add 2 tablespoons shoyu, 1 to 2 teaspoons brown rice or sweet brown rice vinegar, and $1/2$ cup apple juice and cook for 1 more minute.

- 2 tablespoons of mirin may be substituted for the apple juice.

RICE WATER

- Beneficial for diarrhea, painful urination, fevers, and other conditions

Rice water is cool and soothing and traditionally used in India for diarrhea and other bowel trouble, fevers and inflammatory disease, dysuria, and other conditions. It may also be used as an enema. In the United States, a similar remedy was used by the Mormon pioneers who settled in the West.

1. Add $1/2$ ounce of rice to 2 cups of boiling water, reduce heat, and cook for 30 minutes.
2. Strain the liquid.
3. Drink freely, 1 to 2 cups or more

- Add $1/2$ teaspoon of rice syrup to sweeten, if desired.
- Add a little lime juice or drop of lemon or tangerine to stimulate the liver.

RICE WITH WATER-SAUTEED DAIKON AND DAIKON LEAVES

- Beneficial for stomach conditions, including tumors

1. Slice finely 1 cup dried shredded daikon and 1 cup daikon leaves.
2. Sauté with a small volume of water for 15-20 minutes over a low to medium flame.
3. Season lightly with shoyu to taste.
4. Combine vegetables with 2 cups cooked brown rice, mix together well, and let cool for 3 to 4 minutes before eating.

RICE WINE

- Used for festive and religious occasions and medicinally for relaxing contractive disorders

There are a wide variety of alcoholic foods and beverages that are traditionally made with rice, including *mirin* (a sweet cooking wine) and *sake* (a fermented rice wine customarily drunk in tiny glasses).

Mirin

Prepared from rice and koji, a fermented starter, mirin is a clear liquid that may be used to season special dishes and be used to make sauces and dressings. Its enzymes are beneficial for digestion, but its high sugar content (about 30% glucose) and alcohol limit its use to special occasions and conditions. For example, it is not recommended for cancer patients. See RICE VINEGAR (Sweet and Sour Sauce) for a typical recipe that uses mirin.

Sake

Sake, the traditional rice wine of Japan, has spread around the world. It contains about 15% alcohol and has a subtle, but powerful, effect. Only a few small cupfuls may cause dizziness and inebriation. For medicinal use, brown rice sake is preferred. An assortment of "estate sakes" made with polished rice are available in liquor stores and restaurants. Customarily, sake is heated up and drunk hot, though occasionally it is served chilled.

In addition to helping relax a tight, stressful condition, sake will provide warmth, improve circulation, and may be helpful in accidents and emergencies. Those with cancer, liver troubles, and other conditions should strictly avoid.

1. Pour sake into a sake decanter (a small ovoid container) or ceramic cup that can be heated.
2. Place container in a small saucepan, add about 1 inch of water, and gently heat up.
3. When decanter is hot to the touch, take out, and serve in thimbleful size sake cups or other small cup.

ROASTED RICE

- Beneficial for general good health and vitality and many medicinal conditions

Roasted rice is easy to prepare, will keep for several days without refrigeration, and has a delicious nutty texture and taste. After roasting, it can be eaten without further cooking, so it has traditionally been used as an emergency food. It also keeps well during traveling and is very convenient when cooking facilities are not available. Roasted rice may also be made into medicinal teas. See RICE TEA.

1. Dry-roast 1 cup of uncooked brown rice in a skillet over a medium flame for about 10 minutes or until a fragrant aroma is released.
2. Stir with a wooden rice paddle or spoon and shake pan occasionally to prevent burning.
3. Serve plain or with toasted nori, umeboshi plum, scallions, or other condiment.

- Roasted rice will keep without refrigeration for about 5 to 7 days. Keep in a wooden bowl, ceramic container, or for travelling wrap in a cheesecloth bag or baggie.

SPROUTED RICE

- Beneficial for general health as well as relieving tight, contractive conditions, including liver and gallbladder problems

Sprouted rice gives nice light, upward energy and may be used in salads, stir-fries, soups, beverages, and other dishes. It is higher in fiber, minerals, vitamins, lysine (an essential amino acid), and other nutrients than non-germinated rice. But if eaten raw, rice sprouts are not as digestible as cooked rice, so use sparingly or for a specific medicinal purpose. See RICE DRINK (Sprouted Oat-Rice Milk).

1. Obtain a wide-mouth jar or glass canning jar and a screen lid (available in hardware stores or sprouting kits).
2. Place about $1/2$ cup brown rice in the jar, cover with water, and secure lid.
3. Soak for 12 to 18 hours or more.
4. After soaking, invert jar and drain water, then rinse again.
5. Prop jar up at a 45 degree angle for water to drain.
6. Keep out of direct sunlight.
7. Rinse seeds in the jar 2 to 3 times per day, allowing the water to drain on the angle.
8. Sprouts should appear in about 1 to $1\ 1/2$ days. Use as soon as the tiny sprouts or tails appear. If you wait until the root appears, the sprouts may become too bitter. Refrigerate any leftover sprouts and rinse daily.

- White rice will not sprout, so use only whole brown rice. Short or medium grain is recommended. Lundberg Farms "Wehani" rice is preferred by some as the least bitter variety.
- The Chinese traditionally used dried sprouted rice for indigestion, abdominal distension, mouth odor, anorexia, and to stimulate the appetite. After the roots grow to about 1/4 inch in length, dry the sprouts and use as a condiment or garnish or brew into a tea.
- For a very warming preparation, sprout brown rice and roast it, or steam and roast it. Add a little barley malt or rice syrup while roasting. (The steaming makes it more edible.) Instead of a sweet taste, shoyu may be substituted. This is particularly effective to protect against cold weather.

SWEET RICE

- Beneficial for usual good health; for babies, children, and breast-feeding mothers; and for stabilizing blood sugar levels

Sweet rice is a type of glutinous rice commonly known in the East as sticky rice. It is used in making amasake, mochi, ohagis, sake, festive dishes, and other special preparations. Its mild, sweet taste is especially enjoyed by infants, children, and nursing mothers.

Sweet Rice

1. Wash 1 cup sweet rice and put it in a pressure cooker.
2. Add 1 $1/2$ cups water and a pinch of sea salt and follow the basic recipe for PRESSURE-COOKED RICE.
3. Garnish with sliced scallion or parsley.

Sweet Rice Dumplings

1. Place 2 cups sweet rice flour in a mixing bowl.
2. Add 1 cup boiling water and mix.
3. Knead for about 5 minutes and shape the dumplings into any form, keeping the thickness at about $1/2$ inch.
4. Drop the dumplings into the boiling water.
5. When the dumplings rise to the surface, they are done.
6. Serve with clear soup, miso soup, or coat with kinako (roasted soy powder), sesame seeds, or other topping.

VEGETABLE SUSHI

- Beneficial for general good health and for those healing

Vegetable sushi consists of small spirals of seasoned brown rice made with vegetables, tofu, tempeh, noodles, or other ingredients and enclosed with paper-thin strips of nori seaweed. Customarily served with shoyu, grated ginger, and wasabi (Japanese horseradish), brown rice sushi is very delicious and satisfying and suitable for all conditions.

1. Cut 1 carrot in $1/4$-inch lengths and 2 scallions in 8-inch lengths.
2. Blanch the carrot strips and scallions in boiling water for 1 to 2 minutes. Remove and let them cool.
3. Sauté tempeh, cut into thin strips, in a little sesame oil or for those who cannot have oil, water-sauté in some water.
4. Toast 1 sheet of nori by moving it over a medium flame for a few seconds until it turns green.
5. Place the nori on a flat bamboo sushi mat. Rinse your hands with salted water to prevent the rice from sticking and spread about 1 cup of cooked brown rice evenly over the nori leaving about $1/2$ to 1 inch along the top end of the nori and $1/4$ inch at the bottom.
6. With your fingers, make a lengthwise groove in the center of the rice. Place the carrots, tempeh, and scallion greens into the groove in the rice. Spread a small volume of ume paste or sauerkraut along the entire length of the vegetables for seasoning.
7. Roll the sushi mat up, pressing firmly against the rice. Make sure the vegetables are in the center of the roll.
8. To cut, moisten a sharp knife and cut the sushi roll in half and then each half into 2 or 3 pieces. The nori may tear or the rice stick to the knife if the blade is not sharp and wet.
9. After slicing, arrange the rounds on a platter or serving bowl. The cut side with rice and vegetables should be facing up.
10. Serve with shoyu as a dipping sauce, grated ginger, and *wasabi*.

- Traditional favorites from Japan include rice combined separately with cucumber (*kappa-maki*), *kanpyo* (dried gourd), umeboshi plums, natto, chrysanthemum leaves, or tofu skin (*yuba*).
- Seitan, lotus root, and many other plant-quality ingredients may also be used to make sushi.
- For those in good health, white rice sushi may be taken occasionally, though brown rice sushi is preferable. White sushi rice in restaurants often contains sugar and should be avoided.

WHITE RICE

- Beneficial for relaxation, to balance heavy animal food consumption, and for overly contractive conditions

White rice is made by milling whole rice and removing the delicate outer layers, including the germ and the bran. Compared to brown rice, which retains these vitamin and mineral-rich layers, white rice is not recommended for daily or regular consumption. To prevent beriberi, a vitamin B deficiency disease that results from eating polished rice as a staple, nearly all the white rice sold in America today is enriched. However, the nutrients are still less than brown rice, they are easily lost when the rice is rinsed, and the energy of white rice is completely different than that of brown rice.

Historically, white rice was eaten by the aristocracy in Asia and preferred by those in other social classes who were eating strong animal food. The poor (who rarely ate animal food) emulated this pattern with disastrous results. Those who eat meat, eggs, poultry, dairy, and fish are not attracted to dry pressure-cooked brown rice or other whole grains because their livers are tight. They prefer light, polished grains and grain products such as white rice and white flour. That pattern continues today in Japanese and other Asian restaurants where almost all fish and seafood sushi is made with white rice. (Vegetable or vegetarian sushi is preferably made with brown rice since it does not include any animal food.)

Despite the shortcomings of white rice as a regular grain, it can be enjoyed occasionally (once or twice a week) by those in usual good health as an alternative to regular brown rice, or it may be cooked together occasionally with brown rice. Combined with brown rice (in a proportion of half brown and half white rice), it makes for a light, relaxing dish. For overly contractive conditions, such as some prostate and ovarian problems, white rice may be taken more frequently, but only temporarily until the condition improves.

- When buying white rice, obtain organic white rice as much as possible. For sushi, organic sushi rice is also available.
- In Japanese restaurants, ordinary white rice usually contains sugar. To avoid this, ask for "kitchen rice," which is commonly made without sugar.
- To introduce people who are eating in the standard modern way to whole grains, start with softly prepared brown rice or rice cooked into soup.

WILD RICE

- Beneficial for general good health for for most medicinal conditions

Wild rice is an edible wild grass native to North America. It grows from the Midwest to the South and was recently linked by DNA sequencing directly to Asian rice with which it shares a common ancestor. Traditionally, wild rice was harvested in the Great Lakes region by the Ojibwe and other native peoples. Riding in canoes, the harvesters would gently beat the *manoomin* ("the good grain," as it was known) with sticks and gather it from the lakes and rivers. Today, most wild rice is grown in irrigated paddies and is black, shinier, and takes twice as long to cook as native wild rice (50 to 60 minutes instead of 15 to 20 minutes).

Wild rice is expensive (about 5 times as much as ordinary rice), and it is customarily added in small ingredients to brown rice and other grains. It gives a mild, light energy, nutty flavor, and fluffy texture. It is especially nice in salads with corn, green peas, cucumber, and other seasonal vegetables. For medicinal use, the native hand harvested variety is preferred, though it may be difficult to locate. See RICE CROQUETTES (Wild Rice Croquettes with a Mushroom-Onion Sauce).

Rice with Wild Rice

1. Combine 1 cup brown rice and 1/3 cup wild rice with 2 2/3 cups water and a pinch of sea salt. If health permits, a drop of sesame oil may be added for a richer taste.
2. Prepare according to the basic recipe for PRESSURE-COOKED RICE or BOILED RICE.

Popped Wild Rice

This makes a crunchy snack and alternative to popcorn.

1. Warm up 1 to 2 tablespoons sesame oil in a skillet over medium heat.
2. Add 1 cup uncooked wild rice and gently roast until the kernels pop, constantly stirring the rice and occasionally shaking the skillet as a whole.
3. To season, sprinkle a little sea salt or shoyu during roasting.

APPENDIX 1
Dietary Guidelines

The Planetary Health Food Pyramid shows how whole grains, including brown rice, are the foundation of a healthy diet. The pyramid and accompanying dietary guidelines are based on human tradition, climatic and environmental considerations (for a temperate climate), nutritional balance, and other factors. They may require personal modification. The guidelines are compatible with U.S. dietary goals and a balanced macrobiotic, vegetarian, or vegan diet, many traditional ethnic cuisines, and a modern plant-centered way of eating.

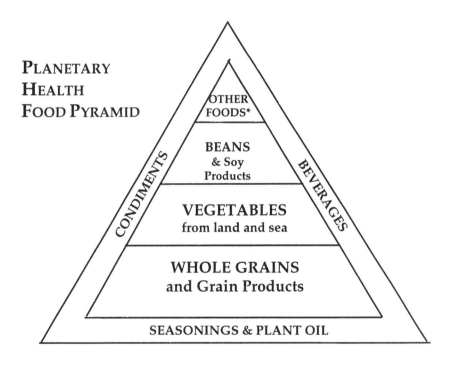

PLANETARY HEALTH FOOD PYRAMID

*Other Foods such as:
Sea Vegetables
Fish and Seafood
Seasonal Fruit
Seeds and Nuts
Natural Snacks
Natural Sweeteners

© 2003 by
Planetary Health, Inc.

1. Whole Grains and Grain Products Approximately half of your daily diet can consist of whole grains, preferably organically grown, non-GE (genetically engineered) varieties. Whole grains include brown rice, barley, millet, whole wheat berries, whole oats, corn, rye, quinoa, and buckwheat. Whole grains are the staff of life. Use them as principal food at each meal. Whenever possible, prepare whole grains daily. Leftovers can be used the following day for breakfast and/or lunch. Whole grain noodles, pasta, Fu (puffed wheat gluten), oatmeal, corn grits, non-yeasted whole sourdough grain bread, and naturally processed grain products are fine for occasional use. Whole grain cookies, crackers, and muffins are best reserved for special occasions, as is seitan (wheat gluten.)

2. Vegetables Vegetables from land and sea can comprise about a third of your daily intake. Seek fresh, organic (non-GE) produce grown in your region. Vegetables can be cooked in a variety of ways. They can be steamed, boiled, sauteed, stir fried, pickled, pressed, deep fried (tempura), grilled, and served raw.

Land vegetables for daily use include roots such as daikon, carrot, turnip, burdock, lotus, parsnip, and radish; round vegetables like winter squash, onion, green cabbage, broccoli, and Brussels sprouts, and leafy greens such as daikon, carrot, and turnip greens, kale, mustard and collard greens, scallion, chive, leek, parsley, and watercress. Shiitake and other mushrooms, green beans, peas, sprouts, summer squash, celery, and lettuce can also be eaten.

Edible sea plants can be included regularly. Preferred varieties include nori, wakame, hiziki, arame, kombu, agar, and dulse. Sea vegetables can be used to add flavor and nutrients to soup, vegetable dishes, salads, and condiments.

3. Beans and Soy Products Beans and soy products can be eaten daily or often in soup, as side dishes, or cooked with rice. Organically grown, non-GE varieties are preferable. Varieties such as azuki, chickpea, and lentil can be used most frequently. Soybean products include tofu (fresh and dried), tempeh, and natto (whole fermented soybeans). Artificial, textured vegetable proteins and soy isolates are best avoided.

Within the regular food categories, soup can be eaten regularly. Fresh organic vegetables, whole grains, beans, noodles, shiitake mushrooms, and nori, wakame, and other sea vegetables are delicious in soup. Soups can be lightly seasoned with organic miso (fermented soy paste), organic shoyu (soy sauce), or white sea salt, and garnished with foods such as sliced scallion, parsley, or chive.

4. Fish and Seafood White meat fish is optional but, if desired, can be eaten several times per week. Look for fresh, non-farm raised seafood. Preferred varieties include cod, haddock, halibut, scrod, trout, red snapper, sole, and flounder. Fish can be garnished with foods such as grated daikon, shoyu, ginger, and lemon. Cooking methods include steaming, boiling, and poaching. Broiled and deep-fried fish can be enjoyed from time to time. Red meat fish and shellfish are best reserved for special occasions. Dried fish flakes, or bonito, can be used on occasion to season broth or as garnish.

- **Seasonal Fruit** Cooked, dried, or fresh fruit can be enjoyed when desired. Local fruits, such as apple, pear, peach, apricot, cherry, fresh local berries, cantaloupe, and watermelon are preferable in temperate zones. Juices made from organic local fruits can be enjoyed on occasion. Tropical fruits are best avoided in temperate zones.
- **Seeds and Nuts** Lightly roasted pumpkin, sesame, and sunflower seeds can be eaten regularly. A small volume of almonds, peanuts, walnuts, pecans, and other nuts can also be eaten as snacks or garnish. Tropical nuts, such as cashew, Brazil, and pistachio, are reserved for special occasions.
- **Natural Snacks** Foods such as leftovers, noodles, vegetarian sushi (brown rice wrapped in nori sea vegetable), and mochi (pounded rice taffy) can be enjoyed regularly. Popcorn, puffed whole cereals, brown rice, sea vegetable, and vegetable chips, and rice cakes can also be enjoyed.
- **Natural Sweeteners** Natural sweeteners such as rice syrup, barley, wheat, and rye malt, amasake (sweet rice milk), and dried chestnuts can be used from time to time in dessert, tea, breakfast cereal, and other dishes.

5. **Seasoning** Unrefined white sea salt is recommended for cooking. Traditionally processed miso and shoyu, prepared from organic (non-GM) soybeans, can also be used to season soup and other dishes. Brown rice and umeboshi (pickled plum) vinegar, mirin (rice cooking wine), lemon, and ginger are also fine.
- **Oil** A moderate amount of unrefined sesame oil can be used regularly in sauteing and stir-frying. Other naturally processed vegetable oils, such as corn, olive, and sunflower, can also be used.

6. **Condiments** A variety of traditional natural condiments can be kept on the table and used to add flavor and nutrients to foods. They can be sprinkled on or added to your dishes. They include: gomashio (sesame salt), shiso (perilla) powder, umeboshi plum, green nori flakes, toasted sesame seeds, tekka root vegetable condiment, kinako (soybean flour), brown rice vinegar, umeboshi vinegar, shoyu , and various combinations of the above.

7. **Beverages** Teas such as bancha, kukicha, barley tea, and brown rice tea can be consumed daily. Organic green tea, corn silk tea, carrot juice, natural amasake, apple juice, and other beverages may also be consumed.

8. **Cooking Tips**
- Select fresh organic ingredients whenever possible.
- Cook with natural spring or well water.
- Use stainless steel, enamel, ceramic, or cast iron pots, skillets, and utensils. Wooden spoons, chopsticks, cutting boards, and bowls are also recommended. Avoid plastic, aluminum, or chemically coated utensils.
- Wash and put away pots, pans, bowls, plates, and other utensils after using. Keep your kitchen clean and orderly.
- Cook on a gas stove or portable gas burner. If necessary, convert from electricity to gas. Avoid microwave ovens.
- Vary ingredients and cooking methods. Experiment with new dishes and recipes. Learn the art of seasonal cooking. Change ingredients and cooking methods if you travel to a different climate. Plan menus daily.
- Cook with a calm, happy, and peaceful mind

APPENDIX 2
The Nutritional Benefits of Rice

Since the Nobel Prize in medicine was awarded in 1929 to Christiaan Eijkman for showing that whole, unprocessed rice could prevent beriberi, the benefits of eating brown rice and other whole grains have been widely recognized. Following is a summary of the nutritional, health, and environmental benefits of whole grain rice:

• **The Food Guide Pyramid Features Brown Rice:** *Dietary Guidelines for Americans*, the booklet that accompanies the U.S. government's food pyramid, recognizes whole grains as the most important category of foods: "Eat foods made from a variety of whole grains—such as whole wheat, brown rice, oats, and whole grain corn—every day." The U.S. government's food recommendations call for whole grains to be the center of each meal, and brown rice is the preferred form in which to eat rice.

• **Brown Rice Aids Digestive Disorders:** In a case-control study, Japanese researchers reported that subjects given a high-fiber, low-protein diet containing brown rice had increased fecal weight, including increased excretion of cholesterol, compared to persons eating a polished rice or other low-fiber diet.[1] Brown rice, containing four times as much dietary fiber as polished rice, significantly increased beneficial bacteria, in the large intestine.[2] Consumption of brown rice (and barley) helped to decrease hepatic glucose production in 10 healthy subjects, Australian scientists reported. Lower glycemic load causes slower release of insulin and helps protect against diabetes and other digestive disorders.[3]

• **Brown Rice Protects Against Heart Disease and High Blood Pressure:** The American Heart Association has long recognized the importance of whole grain rice and other high fiber foods to cardiovascular health. The AHA cookbook includes recipes for brown rice. Harvard scientists reported in the early 1970s that the macrobiotic population in Boston, eating a diet centered on brown rice, had ideal cholesterol levels (average 126 mm Hg) and blood pressure and was virtually at no risk for heart disease.[4] In his classic experiment showing that coronary heart disease could be reversed, Dr. Dean Ornish gave his advanced heart patients a diet centered on brown rice and other whole grains.[5] Eating boiled rice regularly is protective against high blood pressure in Japanese men.[6] A review of five large European cohort studies found that several of the nutrients in grains, including linoleic acid, fiber, vitamin E, selenium, and folate, as well as phytoestrogens of the lignan family and several phenolic acids with antioxidant properties, may reduce the risk of coronary heart disease.[7]

- **Brown Rice Protects Against Cancer:** Women eating brown rice as part of a balanced macrobiotic diet process estrogen more quickly and efficiently than women eating the standard modern diet. Researchers at New England Medical Center concluded this could help prevent breast cancer.[8] Scientists at Tulane University found that patients with pancreatic and prostate cancer who observed a macrobiotic diet high in brown rice and other whole grains lived from two to three times longer than usual cancer patients.[9] In laboratory studies, researchers reported that brown rice and other grains significantly inhibited the development of induced esophageal cancer.[10] Brown rice and other grains high in phytic acid may protect against cancer by suppressing oxidant damage to intestinal epithelium and neighboring cells, according to researchers at the University of Minnesota. The phytochemicals in whole grains further block initial DNA damage and suppress post-initiation processes of tumor development.[11] Brown rice contains inositol hexaphosphate, a natural substance that activates natural killer cell function and inhibits cancer.[12] In tests on human cell lines, British researchers reported that the consumption of brown rice may help protect against breast and colon cancer.[13] In Italy, the National Tumor Institute in Milan reported that a macrobiotic diet high in brown rice could help reduce the risk of breast cancer in high-risk women.[14]

- **Whole Rice Reduces Risk of Diabetes:** White rice and other starchy foods contribute to diabetes, according to Harvard University researchers. A 1997 study of 65,173 women who ate a high starch diet that was low in fiber had 2.5 times as much diabetes as women who consumed whole grains. "Bread, rice, and pasta should be in the whole grain form; brown rice and whole-grain pastas and breads," explained Dr. Walter Willet, professor of epidemiology and nutrition at the Harvard School of Public Health.[15] In an intervention study in Singapore, researchers reported that 183 diabetic patients who took unpolished brown rice, reduced calories, and cut down on oily and fatty food improved self-care and long-term control of the disease compared to 95 patients in the control group.[16]

- **Vitamin B-12 Levels Normal in Children Who Eat Brown Rice:** A nutritional analysis of vegan children 7 to 14 years old who had been eating brown rice for a period of from 4 to 10 years found no symptoms of B12 deficiency compared to an age-matched control group. Other blood values were normal, including red blood cell count, hematocrit, and hemoglobin.[17]

- **Brown Rice in Outer Space:** NASA is developing a special all-plant diet for astronauts featuring brown rice, lentils, seitan, whole wheat tortillas, garden vegetables, and desserts made with amasake, a brown rice-based sweetener. Scientists at Cornell University and Bowling Green State University have developed an all-vegan menu for prolonged space travel from grown hydroponically grown, processed, and prepared in space.

- **Brown Rice Reduces Energy Costs:** The Thai government led a campaign to promote brown rice in 1999 for health and environmental reasons. The national Electricity Generating Authority spearheaded an effort to reduce energy by 60% in the country's 30,000 rice mills, most of which was going to produce white rice. King Bhumiphol, the nation's monarch, endorsed the campaign with a public statement that he eats brown rice. Bangkok supermarkets, restaurants, and Thai airlines now regularly offer brown rice. In the Philippines, scientists reported that converting from white to brown rice would save 65% of total energy required in the milling process.[18]

References

1. K. Kaneko et al., "Effect of Fiber on Protein, Fat, and Calcium Digestibilities and Fecal Cholesterol Excretion," *Journal of Nutrition, Science, and Vitaminology* 32(3):317-25, 1986.

2. Y. Benno" Effect of Rice Fiber on Human Fecal Microflora," *Microbiol Immunol* 33(5):435-40, 1989.

3. A. Thorburn, "Carbohydrate Fermentation Decreases Hepatic Glucose Output in Healthy Subjects," *Metabolism* 42(6):780-5, 1993.

4. F. M. Sacks et al., "Plasma Lipids and Lipoproteins in Vegetarians and Controls," *New England Journal of Medicine* 292:1148-51, 1975.

5. Dean Ornish et al., "Can Lifestyle Changes Reverse Coronary Heart Disease?" *Lancet* 336:129-33, 1990.

6. A. Kanda et al., "Association of Lifestyle Parameters with the Prevention of Hypertension in Elderly Japanese Men and Women," *Asia Pac Journal Public Health* 11(2):77-81, 1999.

7. A. S. Truswell, "Cereal Grains and Coronary Heart Disease," *European Journal of Clinical Nutrition* 56(1):1-14, 2002.

8. B. R. Goldin et al., "Effect of Diet on Excretion of Estrogens in Pre- and Postmenopausal Incidence of Breast Cancer in Vegetarian Women," *Cancer Research* 41:3771-73, 1981.

9. James P. Carter et al, "Hypothesis: Dietary Management May Improve Survival from Nutritionally Linked Cancers Based on Analysis of Representative Cases," *Journal of the American College of Nutrition* 12:209-226, 1983.

10. S. J. van Rensburg et al., "Effects ofVarious Dietary Staples on Esophageal Carcinogeneis Induced in Rats by Subcutaneously Administered N-nitrosomethylbenzylamine," *Journal of the National Cancer Institute* 75(3):561-66, 1985.

11. J. Slavin et al., "Whole Grain Consumption and Chronic Disease: Protective Mechanisms," *Nutrition and Cancer* 27(1):14-21, 1997.

12. *Posit Health News* 17:23-25, 1998.

13. E. A. Hudson et al., "Characterization of Potentially Chemopreventive Phenols in Extracts of Brown Rice that Inhibit the Growth of Human Breast and Colon Cancer Cells," *Cancer Epidemiology, Biomarkers, and Prevention* 9(11):1163-70, 2000.

14. Franco Berrino et al., "Reducing Bioavailable Sex Hormones through a Comprehensive Change in Diet: the Diet and Androgens (DIANA) Randomized Trial," *Cancer Epidemiology, Biomarkers, & Prevention* 10: 25-33, January 2001.

15. Denise Grady, "Diet-Diabetes Link Reported," *New York Times*, February 12, 1997.

16. A. S. Tan, "Patient Education in the Management of Diabetes Mellitus," *Singapore Medical Journal* 38(4):156-60, 1997.

17. H. Suzuki, "Serum Vitamin B12 Levels in Young Vegans Who Eat Brown Rice," *Journal of Nutrition, Science and Vitaminology* 41(6):587-94, 1995.

18. "Brown Rice: Beyond the Color," The Asia Rice Foundation, 2001.

RESOURCES

Amberwaves™ is a network of concerned individuals, families, and communities devoted to preserving rice, wheat, and other essential foods from the threat of genetic engineering, promoting whole grains, and supporting organic farming. Individual membership is $25/year and includes a subscription to the *Amberwaves Journal*, a complimentary book, and other benefits. Amberwaves, P.O. Box 487, Becket, MA 01223, (413) 623-0012, fax (413) 623-6042, www. amberwaves.org; email: info@amberwaves.org

The NOAH Center is a facility where people can gain up to date information on New Opportunities of Alternative Healing. NOAH offers classes in macrobiotic cooking and natural health care, counseling with Alex and Gale Jack, and other programs and activities. NOAH, 401 Stockbridge Road, Great Barrington MA 01230, (413) 528-0297.

Recommended Reading

• Alex Jack and Gale Jack, *Amber Waves of Grain*, paperback, $15.95. A cookbook with 200 recipes drawn from traditional American favorites and contemporary vegetarian, vegan, and macrobiotic cuisine.

• Alex Jack and Edward Esko, editors, *Saving Organic Rice,*, paperback, $6.95. Articles by Dr. Vandana Shiva, Dr. Mae-Wan Ho, and other scientists and environmentalists on the threat of genetically engineered rice.

• Wendy Esko, *Rice Is Nice*, $10.95. 108 delicious, satisfying recipes using brown rice.

Additional copies of Healing with Rice *and the above books, as well as other literature and study materials, are available from the publisher. Please send check or money order payable to "Amberwaves," plus $3.95 postage and handling per shipment to the below address. Bulk rates available to natural foods stores, book stores, educational centers, and other outlets.*

> Amberwaves
> P.O. Box 487
> Becket, MA 01223
> (413) 623-0012
> Fax (413) 623-6042
> Email: info@amberwaves.org

ABOUT THE AUTHORS

Alex Jack, an author, teacher, and dietary counselor, served as a reporter in Vietnam in the 1960s, editor-in-chief of the *East West Journal* in the 1970s, general manager of the Kushi Foundation in the 1980s, and director of the One Peaceful World Society in the 1990s. He has taught around the world, including the Zen Temple in Beijing, the Cardiology Center in Leningrad, and in Europe and Japan. He is the author, co-author, or editor of thirty-five books, including *The Cancer Prevention Diet, Diet for a Strong Heart,* and *The Macrobiotic Path to Total Health* (with Michio Kushi), *Complete Guide to Macrobiotic Cooking* (with Aveline Kushi), *Let Food Be Thy Medicine*, and *The Mozart Effect* (with Don Campbell). Alex is president of Planetary Health/Amberwaves. He actively teaches and counsels around the world.

Gale Jack taught elementary school and served as a psychological counselor in the Houston and Dallas public schools for many years. She has served as co-founder of the Heart-of-Texas Macrobiotic Center in Dallas and the associate director of the Kushi Institute. She is the author or editor of several books, including *Promenade Home, Amber Waves of Grain, Women's Health Guide,* and *Raising Healthy Pets*. She has written for *Macrobiotics Today,* Cybermacro, and other print and online publications. The mother of two children and grandmother of one, Gale is on the board of directors of Planetary Health/Amberwaves, teaches medicinal cooking, and gives personal guidance and advice.

Counseling with Alex and Gale

Alex and Gale are certified macrobiotic counselors and teachers and offer dietary and way of life consulations, guidance on home remedies, and personal tutorials on macrobiotics in person, by telephone, or by email. For further information, please contact:

> Alex and Gale Jack
> 305 Brooker Hill Road
> Becket, MA 01223
> Telephone (413) 623-0012
> Fax (413) 623-6042
> Alex's email: shenwa@bcn.net
> Gale's email: galejack@msn.com

INDEX OF CONDITIONS AND DISORDERS

Accidents, 59, 78
Allergies, 36, 38
Anemia, 20, 26, 27, 28, 30
Animal food, excess intake, 11, 83
Anorexia, 80
Appetite, stimulation of, 22, 80
Arthritis, 27, 30, 64, 72
Babies, 53, 61
Bladder, 31, 73. *See also kidney.*
Blood strengthening, 28, 34
Blood sugar, 75, 81
Body and mouth odor, 21, 46, 61, 73, 80
Boils, 38
Bone and joint disorders, 27, 45, 51, 52, 55, 58, 64
Bones, broken, 22, 38
Brain disorders, 74
Breast problems, 15, 66
Breastfeeding, 26, 44, 52, 55, 61, 81
Bronchitis, 74
Burns, 65, 66
Childhood conditions, 44, 55, 69, 81
Circulatory, 16, 20, 23, 28, 30, 43, 50, 62, 75, 78
Coldness, 20, 21, 23, 26, 27, 47, 68
Colds, 49, 59
Colitis, 34
Colon cancer, 73
Congenital defects, 61
Congestion, 64
Constipation, 16
Contractive conditions, 47, 71, 74, 78, 80, 83
Cough, 49, 71
Cravings for sweets, 12, 13
Cuts and wounds, 56
Depression, 12, 13

Diabetes, 25, 29, 62
Diarrhea, 16, 76
Digestive problems, 16, 18, 19, 23, 37, 43, 47, 59, 73, 78
Dizziness, 30
Down syndrome, 44, 52, 55
Ear and hearing, 35
Eczema, 36
Energy, lack of, 20, 28, 45
Environmental illness, 30
Erysipelas, 66
Expansive conditions, 48
Eye problems, 33
Fat and oil, excess of, 63, 73
Fever, 59, 76
Flu, 49, 59
Frostbite, 20
Gallbladder. *See Liver and gallbladder.*
Grinding of teeth, 12, 13
Headache, 58
Heart troubles, 20, 43, 62
Hives, 38
Hypoglycemia, 12, 13, 25, 29, 62
Immune disorders, 16, 34
Infections, 38
Infectious disease, 25, 34
Infertility, 11. 26
Inflammation, 56, 58, 65
Ingrown toenail, 22
Insomnia, 26, 63
Intestinal problems, 19, 31, 37, 43, 46, 73,
Irregular heartbeat, 20
Itching, 36, 56
Kidney and bladder problems, 11, 31, 35, 51, 52, 72
Knee and ankle problems, 58

Leukemia, 11, 29, 30
Liver and gallbladder, 14, 19, 22, 31, 62, 75, 80
Low energy, 20
Lung problems, 31, 49, 53
Lymphatic conditions, 25, 62, 64
Menstrual cramps, 13
Miscarriage, 34
Mood swings, 12, 13
Morning sickness, 59, 61, 70
Motion sickness, 23
Mouth odor. *See Body and mouth odor.*
Natural beauty, 24, 66
Nausea, 23
Nervous conditions, 16, 28
Obesity, 71
Ovarian problems, 11, 15, 62, 74
Overweight, 12, 13, 21, 71
Pancreatic problems, 17, 25, 31, 62, 75
Peaceful mind, 31
Poison ivy, 38
Pregnancy, 27, 52, 58, 59
Pregnancy poisoning, 27, 61
Prostate problems, 11, 15, 62
Prostate cancer, 30, 52
Radiation, 34
Rashes, 38
Relaxation, 83
Reproductive, 11

Respiratory conditions, 31, 49, 53, 74
Retardation, 11
Sadness, 26
Scalds, 65, 66
Shoulder and neck aches, 58, 61
Sinusitis, 74
Skin cancer, 54
Skin care, 24
Skin conditions, 36, 38, 54, 66
Sleeping problems, 30
Sore throat, 23
Spiritual development, 48
Spleen problems, 17, 18, 25, 31, 62, 75
Sprains, 22
Stomach problems, 16, 17, 22, 25, 31, 37, 62, 77
Strength, 34, 37, 44, 48
Stress, 12, 13, 26, 71, 78
Stroke, 44
Surgery, 44
Swelling, 56
Tumors, 63, 64
Underweight, 24, 26
Urination, excessive, 76
Uterine cancer, 64
Varicose veins, 20
Vitality, 34, 37, 44, 48, 50, 64, 68
Warmth, 20, 21, 23, 26, 27, 47, 68, 78
Worms and parasites, 33
Wrinkling, 66

INDEX OF RECIPES AND REMEDIES

Soft Grain and Porridges
Congee 18
Ojiya 30
Rice Cream 44
Rice Porridge 59
    Fresh Soft Porridge 59
    Porridge with Leftover Rice 60
    Miso Rice Porridge 60
    Rice Porridge with Aduki Beans 61
    Rice Porridge with Bancha Tea 61
    Rice Porridge with Barley 62
    Rice Porridge with Corn 62
    Rice Porridge with Grated Daikon 62
    Rice Porridge with Grated Lotus Root 62
    Rice Porridge with Millet 63
    Rice Porridge with Squash 64
    Sweet Rice Porridge 64
    Rice Porridge with Millet, Buckwheat, and Vegetables 64
    Roasted Rice Porridge 64
Soft Barley Rice 14
Soft Millet Rice 25

Rice Soups and Broths
Brown Rice Soup 68
Miso Soup with Mochi 28
Rice Soup with Lotus Seeds 53
Thunder Tea Soup 68

Grain Dishes
Barley Rice 14
Boiled Rice 16
    Omo or African Style Rice 16
Fried Rice 20
Hato-Mugi Rice 24
Millet Rice 25
Pressure-Cooked Rice 31
Raw Rice 33
Roasted Rice 79
Rice with Corn 43
Rice Croquettes 45
    Wild Rice Croquettes with a Mushroom-Onion Sauce 45
Rice Fast 48
Rice with Lotus Seeds 53
Sprouted Rice 80
Sweet Rice 81
White Rice 83
Wild Rice 84

Rice and Bean, Seed, or Nut Dishes
Aduki Bean Rice 11
Black Soybean Rice 15
Chestnut Rice 17
Rice with Beans 35

Rice and Vegetable Dishes
Rice with Daikon Pickles 46
Rice Gomoku 50
Rice with Marinated Dried Daikon 54
Rice with Water-Sautéed Daikon and Daikon Leaves 77
Rice Bran Pickles 37

Rice Balls, Cakes, and Spirals
Mochi 26
    Pan-fried 26
    Fried 27
    in Bancha Tea 27

in Miso Soup	28
Ohagi	29
Rice Balls	34
Rice Cakes	41
Sweet Rice Cakes	41
Small Fried Rice Cakes	42
Sweet and Savory Rice Cakes	42
Vegetable Sushi	82

Rice Bread, Noodles, and Dumplings

Carolina Rice and Wheat Bread	40
Idli Steamed Bread	19
Rice Kayu Bread	39
Rice Noodles in Broth	57
Sweet Rice Dumplings	81

Rice Seasonings and Condiments

Mirin	78
Rice Vinegar	75
Sweet and Sour Sauce	75

Rice Snacks and Desserts

Amasake Pudding	67
Popped Wild Rice	84
Rice Cakes	41
Small Fried Rice Cakes	41
Rice Pudding	67
Rice Syrup	71

Rice Beverages and Teas

Amasake	12
Ame Kuzu Tea	13
Fermented Rice Drink	19
Fermented Rice Drink Sweetened with Barley Malt	47
Genshin Tea	21
Ginger Tea with Rice	23
Rice Drink	47
Sikya	47
Sprouted Oat-Rice Milk	47
Rice Juice	51
Rice Liquid	52
Rice Milk	55
Rice Tea	72
Rice Tea with Aduki Beans, Dried Daikon, and Shiitake	72
Rice Tea with Dried Daikon Daikon Leaves, and Shiitake	73
Rice Tea with Dried Daikon, Daikon Leaves, Shiitake, and Dried Lotus Root	73
Rice Tea with Dried Daikon, Kombu, and Shiitake	73
Rice Tea with Dried Daikon, Shiitake, and Cabbage	74
Rice Tea with Lotus Root	74
Rice with Green Tea	74
Roasted Rice Tea	72
Rice Water	76
Rice Wine	78
Saké	78

Rice Compresses and Other External Applications

Ginger-Scallion-Rice Wine Compress	22
Raw Rice Plaster	56
Rice Bran Compress	36
Rice Bran Plaster	38
Rice-Ginger Compress	49
Rice-Miso Plaster	56
Rice Pack	58
Rice Powder	65
Rice Poultice	66
Rice Flour Poultice	66
Skin and Beauty Poultice	66